FRANK LLOYD WRIGHT'S HOLLYHOCK HOUSE

DONALD HOFFMANN

DOVER PUBLICATIONS, INC., NEW YORK

Hollyhock House is a property of the Department of Recreation and Parks of the City of Los Angeles. Sited in Barnsdall Park, at 4808 Hollywood Boulevard, the house is operated by the Cultural Affairs Department and is regularly open for guided tours. Those who plan a visit should telephone for tour hours: (213) 662–7272.

Published in Canada by General Publishing Company, Ltd.,
30 Lesmill Road, Don Mills, Toronto, Ontario.
Published in the United Kingdom by Constable and Company, Ltd.,
3 The Lanchesters, 162–164 Fulham Palace Road,
London W6 9ER.

Frank Lloyd Wright's Hollyhock House is a new work, first published by Dover Publications, Inc., in 1992.

Manufactured in the United States of America
Dover Publications, Inc.
31 East 2nd Street
Mineola, N.Y. 11501

Library of Congress Cataloging-in-Publication Data

Hoffmann, Donald.
Frank Lloyd Wright's Hollyhock House / Donald Hoffmann.
p.   cm.
Includes index.
ISBN 0-486-27133-1
1. Wright, Frank Lloyd, 1867–1959—Criticism and interpretation.
2. Hollyhock House (Museum)   3. Los Angeles (Calif.)—Buildings,
structures, etc.   I. Title.
NA737.W7H62   1992
728.8′092—dc20   92-24841
CIP

PREFACE AND ACKNOWLEDGMENTS

HOLLYHOCK HOUSE wins friends and admirers, but as a work of art is little understood and greatly underestimated. The complexity and strength of the house can be sensed from a curious fact: It is portrayed with equal accuracy in the vague photographic reveries of Viroque Baker, from the early years, and in the photographs Ezra Stoller made in March 1954, so clear and handsome.

The study presented here derives almost entirely from primary documents and direct observation. It was undertaken at the invitation of Virginia Ernst Kazor, the devoted curator of Hollyhock House, and Roderick Grant, an exceptionally knowledgeable volunteer. I am indebted first of all to them and to Clark Pardee, volunteer archivist and researcher, who offered his time and the details of his findings with great generosity. I am grateful as well for the kindnesses of Muffet Hendricks, secretary at the house. Besides the full support and advice of those who have cared most for Hollyhock House, I was fortunate in having financial assistance from the Cultural Affairs Department of the City of Los Angeles and the rare opportunity to live in and with the house, day and night, for three weeks.

Hollyhock House was conceived and built under difficult conditions. Those same circumstances, however, led to a wealth of documentation, visual and verbal, that now reposes in the Frank Lloyd Wright Archives at Taliesin West, in the R. M. Schindler Collection at the University Art Museum of the University of California, Santa Barbara, and in the archives of the house itself. Bruce Brooks Pfeiffer, Indira Berndtson and Oscar Munoz of the Frank Lloyd Wright Archives provided quick and courteous cooperation. Occasionally, my transcriptions of letters relating to Hollyhock House vary slightly from those previously published; faded ink, hasty handwriting, alterations and interlineations make some of the correspondence difficult to transcribe. The letters of Frank Lloyd Wright to Aline Barnsdall dated September 24, 1920, and June 27, 1921, are copyright © The Frank Lloyd Wright Foundation 1986. Those of March 3, 1923, to Louis H. Sullivan and February 26, 1932, to Henry-Russell Hitchcock are copyright © The Frank Lloyd Wright Foundation 1984. All others are copyright © The Frank Lloyd Wright Foundation 1992.

An article by Kathryn Smith on "Frank Lloyd Wright, Hollyhock House, and Olive Hill, 1914–1924" in the March 1979 issue of the *Journal of the Society of Architectural Historians* laid the groundwork for further study of the house.

For their kind help, I wish to thank Neil Levine of Harvard University; Marc F. Wilson of the Nelson-Atkins Museum of Art; Brent Sverdloff of the Archives of the History of Art, the Getty Center; David Gebhard of the University of California, Santa Barbara; Eric Lloyd Wright of Malibu, California; James Helyar of the Spencer Research Library at the University of Kansas; Linda Hill of the Los Angeles Public Library; M. Guy Bishop of the Natural History Museum of Los Angeles County; Deborah Barlow of the Architecture and Fine Arts Library at the University of Southern California; William J. Delehanty of the Paul Weigel Library of Architecture and Design at Kansas State University, Manhattan; Noel Millea of *L.A. Architect*; Carolyn D. Koenig of *Architectural Record*; and J. Kevin O'Brien of the Federal Bureau of Investigation. I also benefited from the resources of the Benson Memorial Library and the library of the Drake Well Museum, both in Titusville, Pennsylvania; the library of the Historical Society of Western Pennsylvania, in Pittsburgh; the Carnegie Library of Pittsburgh; and the Miller Nichols Library at the University of Missouri at Kansas City.

It is a pleasure to thank my son Michael J. Hoffmann, Elizabeth A. Kline, Kenneth La Fave, Edgar Tafel, John Hoffmann, Robert Kostka, Sarah Landau, Mosette Broderick, Diane Thomas, Erica Stoller, Richard Hollander, Robert Wojtowicz and Myriam Young. I am particularly grateful for the encouragement of Fred B. Hoffmann, Stanley Appelbaum, Henry Adams, Helen Ashmore, Ellen Goheen, Victoria Spain, Lenore K. Bradley, Pamela D. Kingsbury and, most of all, Robin Jefferies Younger.

D. H.

CONTENTS

LIST OF ILLUSTRATIONS

1. Hollyhock House, west front. (Ezra Stoller © Esto)

DREAMS

ALINE BARNSDALL AND FRANK LLOYD WRIGHT arrived in Los Angeles by the same route, driven by parallel ambitions. Miss Barnsdall, as she was always called, meant to launch a new theater that could regenerate the American stage. Wright wanted to invent an indigenous American architecture, suited especially to southern California and perhaps the entire Southwest. To such ambitions, success is seldom granted; but from this highminded association of client and architect there came at least a strange and wonderful residence. Miss Barnsdall called it "Hollyhocks," after her favorite flower. Wright, in time, named it Hollyhock House, by which it is known still today [Fig. 1].

Hollyhock House rises from an isolated hill in east Hollywood. It stands alone, as well, among the hundreds of buildings that Wright conceived during his long and extraordinarily fertile career. Stately and yet endearing, even playful, the house is all at once an oasis, paradise garden, rooftop promenade, lookout and retreat. It is also a theater for the performance each day of sun and shadow, a place of peculiar enchantment [2]. Hollyhock House was built in 1920–21, a most difficult and awkward time in the architect's life. But his correspondence, his autobiography, the drawings and indeed the house itself all agree on something else: that he put into it much of himself and the best that he had to give. Wright called Hollyhock House his "California Romanza."[1]

Architecture asks first for a client, and at first Miss Barnsdall must have seemed the client of an architect's dreams. She was a woman of large means and many affections [3]. She liked dogs, she liked flowers, she liked radical causes, all the arts and especially the theater. Most of all, she liked to travel. Miss Barnsdall was not adept at getting along with people; she once wrote Wright that she had always put "climate and natural beauty" before people. When things did not go her way she simply went somewhere else. This unsettled way of life rendered paradoxical any relation she might have to architecture, the least movable of the arts. What qualified her as a great client was her access to great wealth. It came directly from her father, whose wealth came directly from the earth.

Theodore Newton Barnsdall was an independent oil operator and financier of daunting energies [4]. Most often remembered for being always on the move, he kept bank accounts in eight states, and people called him T. N., as though even his name had to be rushed. When he died at his home in Pittsburgh, the morning newspaper said he had been an indefatigable worker, often too busy to sit down for a meal, and that "it was not an uncommon sight to see him emerging from a restaurant in the Diamond munching a huge bologna sandwich as he hurried along to keep an appointment or attend to some business matter."[2] A huge sand-

---

[1] Wright, *An Autobiography* (New York, 1932), p. 225. All references to his autobiography unless otherwise noted will be to this first edition.

[2] *The Gazette Times* (Pittsburgh), Feb. 28, 1917, p. 2. His death was also reported in *The Pittsburgh Press* and the *New York Times* of that date, and on March 3 in the weekly *Bulletin* of Pittsburgh.

3. Aline Barnsdall in Los Angeles.

2. Pool and garden court, early 1920s; looking predominantly west.

4. Memorial to T. N. Barnsdall at Hollyhock House.

wich for a huge man, six feet four inches tall and 250 pounds. A trade journal said Barnsdall had been the most restless personality in the petroleum industry: "Three-quarters of this operator's time was spent on railroads and on other means of conveyance . . . he was virtually homeless."[3]

He had such a knack for oil that the Standard Oil Company, between 1905 and 1907, with rare benevolence toward an independent, underwrote his operations in the Oklahoma field with interest-free loans of $7.5 million.[4] T. N. Barnsdall was born to oil, it is fair to say, because the place of his birth, a pleasantly wooded and obscure town named Titusville, in northwestern Pennsylvania, so soon became the birthplace of the petroleum industry. His father, William Barnsdall, was born in 1810 in Bedfordshire, England, and had settled into Titusville in the 1830s. The elder Barnsdall quickly sensed the potential profit in oil, an insight that

strangely eluded Edwin Laurentine Drake, the former rail-road conductor from New Haven, Connecticut, whose rude derrick performed the first successful drilling for rock-oil, or petroleum, in August 1859. Drake had arrived in Titusville with calculated flourish, calling himself a colonel. He began drilling not far south of town, and endured great ridicule during the long months before his well came in. The very next year he was content to be elected a justice-of-the-peace.

William Barnsdall, by contrast, gave up his trade of shoe-making and, for a time, the farm north of town to which he had walked every day from his home. With several partners, he began to drill on the farm of his brother-in-law, a quarter of a mile north of the Drake well and nearer to town. Soon the Barnsdall well became the second successfully drilled oil well in the world. Sunk much deeper, it came into full operation in February 1860. Later that year, William Barns-dall became a partner in building the first oil refinery. Rock-oil, known even in ancient times, had long been skimmed from ponds and random seepages. It was sold in America as snake-oil, for treating all manner of bodily complaints, or as

    3 William S. Bredin, "The Incomparable Operator," in *The Oil and Gas Man's Magazine*, Apr. 1917, p. 101.
    4 *New York Times*, Dec. 3, 1908, p. 18 and Dec. 10, 1908, p. 1; also, *The Petroleum Gazette*, Dec. 1908, p. 2.

a lubricant for machinery. Oil drawn from deep in the earth proved plentiful, and could now take the place of whale oil as a source of the notable illuminant kerosene.[5]

T. N. Barnsdall, born on June 10, 1851, was eight years old when Colonel Drake struck oil. Only the dimmest of Titusville lads could have ignored the excitement of 1859–

60. T. N. Barnsdall worked first at one of his father's wells at a place south of Titusville ingloriously named Pit Hole, now happily vanished. He was 16 when he drilled his first well, with help from his father. A glass-plate photograph from that year, 1867, captures the humble origins of the Barnsdall fortune [5]. The boom in Titusville lasted nearly a decade, but William Barnsdall already was drilling at the west edge of Bradford, 75 miles to the northeast and almost into the state of New York. In the 1870s the Bradford field grew famous. (Today, the oldest active well from that time can be discovered downtown, behind McDonald's; it yields a barrel of crude oil a day.) T. N. Barnsdall also began drilling at Bradford, where he negotiated valuable leases. He rented an office downtown and kept rooms nearby. In 1880 he finally moved

5 For the early history of the oil industry and the Barnsdalls, see J. T. Henry, *The Early and Later History of Petroleum* (Philadelphia, 1873); *History of Crawford County, Pennsylvania* (Chicago, 1885); John J. McLaurin, *Sketches in Crude-Oil* (Franklin, Pa., 1896); Paul H. Giddens, *The Birth of the Oil Industry* (New York, 1938); Ida M. Tarbell, *All in the Day's Work* (New York, 1939); Harold F. Williamson and Arnold R. Daum, *The American Petroleum Industry: the Age of Illumination 1859–1899* (Evanston, Ill., 1959); Richard Foy and Alice Morrison, *Titusville of Yesterday* (Oil City, Pa., 1984), and the *National Cyclopaedia of American Biography*, vol. 26 (New York, 1937), pp. 458–59, and vol. 35 (New York, 1949), p. 470.

5. Barnsdall offices in Shamburg, Pa., 1867.

6. Aline Barnsdall (left) and her sister Frances, 1899.

to Bradford. The following year, on June 22, he married Louisa Angela Stitt. Angie, as she was called, had been born on April 23, 1854, in the town of Meadville, about 25 miles west of Titusville. Their first child was born in Bradford on April 1, 1882, in their modest home on Walker Avenue. They named her Louisa Aline.

Within a few years, T. N. Barnsdall took offices in Pittsburgh, and by 1893 he had moved there. About ten years later, he bought a mansion that occupied a site extending along North Negley Avenue more than 490 feet north from Wellesley Avenue. Among its other amenities were a music room, library and porte-cochere, or carriage porch—features that Miss Barnsdall would have as well in Hollyhock House.[6] Despite his wealth, his mansion and, indeed, his size, T. N. Barnsdall avoided the public eye. A book honoring the most successful and wealthy men in Pittsburgh managed only to provide his name and an engraved portrait, with no biographical sketch whatever. Government attorneys investigating Standard Oil failed to identify him for more than a year, and during the hearings in New York they spoke mockingly of "the mysterious Mr. Barnsdall" as though he perhaps did not even exist.[7]

Barnsdall borrowed heavily, took large risks, built a reputation for keeping his word, stayed in good humor and bore his failures with enviable ease, although a major reversal may have contributed to his final illness. (Before Oklahoma was admitted as a state in 1907, he ventured into Indian Territory and secured leases on some 334,000 acres of potential oil and natural-gas lands; less than ten years later, he was ordered by the government to relinquish his leases on all but 4,800 acres.) Even so, Barnsdall at the end of his life controlled about 20 companies, some of which were mines for gold, silver, zinc, lead, iron and coal. Adventurous, private and not much concerned with courting the esteem of others, he could have seen all those traits reflected in his daughter Aline [6].

The generous allowance he gave her also became a formative element in her life. Before the outbreak of World War I, she spent much of her time in Europe. Her path to Wright in fact began in Berlin, and not because of the great portfolio of his work published there in 1910 by Ernst Wasmuth. Early in 1913, a friend introduced her there to young Lawrence Langner, already an international patent agent and soon to become a playwright and theatrical manager as well. They fell in love. Much later, Langner disguised her as "Celeste" in his memoirs:

Celeste was neither fair nor dark, though her light-brown hair, blue eyes and transparent skin made one remember her as a blond rather than a brunette. She was a creature of great enthusiasms, and had a habit of growing so excited over them that she often choked up and became both breathless and speechless, and would have to let her eyes and facial expression finish her sentences for her. She was a few years older than I, but we were the same age in our enthusiasm over the theatre and Bernard Shaw, and she was even younger when it came to discussing politics and Victorian morality, against which she was in even greater revolt than I was . . .

Celeste, like myself, had become infatuated with the productions at the Deutsches Theater, and wanted to see plays presented in this new way in the American theatre. From the time she had been a young girl, she had fallen in love with the theatre . . . .[8]

After an idyll in the Bavarian Alps—Miss Barnsdall used a Baedeker to choose a mountain where she meant to consummate the relationship—Langner returned to New York,

[6] An outline of the mansion in relation to the site appears in the *Real Estate Plat-Book of the City of Pittsburgh* (Philadelphia, 1939), vol. 3, plate 10. The site, consisting of lots 138 and 169 of block 82K, is occupied today by a group of garden-apartment buildings comprising 145 units.

[7] *New York Times*, Dec. 3, 1908, p. 18. The government argued that the loan arrangement with Barnsdall gave Standard Oil absolute control over his operations in Oklahoma. The town of Barnsdall, Oklahoma, is named for the Barnsdall Oil Co., which no longer exists.

[8] Lawrence Langner, *The Magic Curtain* (New York, 1951), pp. 58, 59 and 63; subsequent extracts are from pp. 73 and 83. Langner (1890–1962) helped found both the Washington Square Players and the Theatre Guild in New York. His amusing autobiography belies Norman Bel Geddes' assertion that he had no sense of humor.

where he and his brother had an apartment in Greenwich Village:

My life in the Village was periodically interrupted by my life with Celeste, which turned out to be a series of railroad jumps broken by journeys to many of the mountainous sections of the United States, where she indulged her passion for seeing what was on the other side of the range. Celeste lived in four homes, all inconveniently situated several hundred miles apart . . . I did my best to induce her to settle in New York, but was unsuccessful, for Celeste felt cramped by its buildings, and bewildered by its vibrations. She gasped for spiritual air . . . .

Langner soon opened a branch office of his patent business in Chicago. Because he found most Broadway plays cheap and meretricious, he was delighted to be introduced to the Chicago literary scene and to discover the Chicago Little Theater, pioneered by the poet Maurice Browne and his wife, the actress Ellen Van Volkenburg:

The fact that Maurice Browne was able to exist at all in Chicago made a great impression upon me, and I wrote to Celeste telling her that if an Art Theatre of this kind was possible in Chicago, it would be even more possible in New York. Celeste, who never permitted anyone else to do her thinking for her, decided exactly the opposite, and immediately rushed to Chicago and she opened her first play there, presumably on the theory that two art theatres could starve as easily as one.

In 1912 Browne and his wife had leased a fourth-floor back space in the Fine Arts Building on Michigan Avenue, which they transformed into a theater with 91 seats and a 14-foot stage. It was to be a little theater, Browne recalled, because "a small theatre would cost less than a large one."[9] Among the first of their players was Elaine Hyman, an Art Institute student who soon began an affair with the novelist Theodore Dreiser. Later, after moving East and taking the stage name of Kirah Markham, she moved West to join Miss Barnsdall's theater company in Los Angeles, where she met Lloyd Wright, the architect's eldest son, and married him.

Aline Barnsdall and Frank Lloyd Wright met in Chicago. Henry Blackman Sell, who like Wright was a native of southern Wisconsin, was the person who introduced them, Wright recalled. Sell was related to the showman William F. ("Buffalo Bill") Cody; much later, he wrote a book with Victor Weybright titled *Buffalo Bill and the Wild West*. As a young journalist and man-about-town, Sell kept abreast of the brief

Chicago renaissance. Soon he became literary editor of the *Chicago Daily News*. He admired Wright's accomplishment in the Midway Gardens, a festive entertainment place near the southeast corner of Washington Park. "Here the artist and his dream have come near a meeting," Sell wrote, "and for the first time in many, many years the forms of three arts, architecture, sculpture and painting, are found proceeding from and determined by the same mind."[10]

Wright said his introduction to Miss Barnsdall took place at his apartment on Cedar Street, close by the Lake Shore Drive; but Miss Barnsdall recalled that they met five or six blocks to the north, at the most famous house in Chicago. "You should never be apologized for, even with love in the heart," she wrote him in June 1946, after she read John Lloyd Wright's memoir *My Father Who Is on Earth*, "because people either understand at once and accept you with admiration & respect, as I did that evening in Mrs. Potter Palmer's garage, or they just haven't the imagination or freedom of heart to ever understand." Much more important than the place of their meeting, or why they may have been in Mrs. Palmer's garage, was the time. Wright said it was not long after the tragedy at Taliesin, his country home and studio near Spring Green, Wisconsin. That would have been late in 1914; in August, a disturbed servant set the house afire and killed seven persons before they could flee. Among the victims were Wright's companion Mamah Cheney and her two children. The prospect of building the Imperial Hotel in Tokyo, and now the chance to do important work for Miss Barnsdall, came as if godsends to turn his mind and will to the future.

Norman Bel Geddes, the precocious and spirited designer, left a vivid picture of the early years of Wright and Miss Barnsdall. Around the turn of the century, Geddes (as he was known more plainly before 1916, when he married a young woman named Belle and was inspired to redesign his own name) spent a few childhood years in the best part of Pittsburgh, like Miss Barnsdall. His family lived next door to Harry K. Thaw, the very same who was to marry the showgirl Evelyn Nesbit—herself a native of Tarentum, just northeast of Pittsburgh—and later, in the rooftop theater in Madison Square Garden, was to murder the architect Stanford White in much-delayed revenge for what Thaw considered assaults upon his wife's premarital honor. Geddes was as self-taught as he was self-propelled, but he studied a little at the Cleveland Institute of Art and at the Art Institute of Chicago. He made friends in Cleveland with a Blackfoot

---

[9] Maurice Browne, *Too Late to Lament: An Autobiography* (Bloomington, Ind., 1956), p. 111.

[10] Henry Blackman Sell, "Interpretation not Imitation," *International Studio*, May 1915, supp. pp. 79–83. In 1920 Sell (1889–1974) became editor of what was then called *Harper's Bazar*; later, he had great success in marketing "Sell's Liver Paté." For many years he was prominent in New York cafe society.

named Thundercloud, an artist's model of some renown, and questioned him about the Indian legend of the enormous prehistoric Thunderbird. In the summer of 1912, Geddes traveled to the Blackfeet Indian Reservation in northwest Montana, sketched the Indians and tried to learn more about the great bird. A few years later, in Detroit, where he was making a name as a poster designer, Geddes wrote a play titled *Thunderbird*. And it was because of *Thunderbird* that he came to the attention of Miss Barnsdall.

Geddes met her through the composer Charles Wakefield Cadman, best remembered for his popular tune "From the Land of the Sky-blue Water," a love song based on an Omaha tribal melody. Cadman, too, took great interest in Indians. He had studied music in Pittsburgh, where he served a few years as music critic of the *Dispatch*. Cadman not only was an exact contemporary of Miss Barnsdall's, but a friend. He gave lecture-recitals of Indian music, and wrote about "idealizing the only existent form of folk-song indigenous to American soil."[11] Much sentiment about Indians was in the air. Wright, in searching for the indigenous, had long been fascinated by Indians—a fact Miss Barnsdall seemed not to grasp until 30 years later.

A year or so after Wright and Miss Barnsdall met, Geddes learned that Cadman was to perform in Ann Arbor, Michigan. Cadman, he thought, would be just the person to write music for *Thunderbird*. He arranged to meet Cadman and leave the manuscript with him:

A few days later a letter came from Cadman saying he was intrigued by the play and would like to do the music, but only when I had a production contract. His letter mentioned a Miss Aline Barnsdall, who had produced *Alice in Wonderland* in Chicago and New York the previous winter [1914–15], and who wanted to produce plays on American themes. He said he would be seeing her in Pittsburgh and would show her the play.[12]

Geddes waited two months for Cadman to arrive in Detroit for another recital, then entertained Cadman at his home by performing *Thunderbird* on his ingenious miniature stage:

That clinched it. He got off a long telegram to Miss Barnsdall in Pittsburgh telling her he was so impressed he had signed a contract with me to do the music. Miss Barnsdall's answer bounced right back: ARRIVING TO-MORROW TO TAKE OPTION ON THUNDERBIRD.

I met her at the door. "Tell your father," she said to me, "that Aline Barnsdall is here." She was surprised, but not disappointed, to learn that I was the right Norman Geddes. She was interesting-looking, even fascinating, but without beauty. She immediately inquired if she could see a model performance of *Thunderbird*. I did the show for her and her reactions were delightful. She laughed and clapped with glee. But when it was over she became quite serious.

"I want you to know about my plans for a permanent experimental theater organization. Its purpose will be the development of American talent in writing, acting, staging, and everything else that is a part of the creative theater."

"In New York?" I asked.

"I loathe New York," she said angrily. "Detest it. It is the worst possible place for creative people. Please don't mention it again."

Miss Barnsdall took special pride in choosing associates. "Any impression that I have made has not been thru the money I have expended," she wrote Wright in November 1927. "It has been in my *original* impulse and discrimination in choosing the right people for the work." Wright's reputation was at low ebb when she told Geddes that she had retained the finest architect in America; moreover, she hired Geddes as her stage designer when he was only 22 and without a single public theatrical production to his credit. He succeeded Jerome Blum, a friend of Wright's whose portrait of Maurice Browne hung near the foyer of the Chicago Little Theater. Miss Barnsdall also hired Richard Ordynski, a Polish actor and stage manager who had been working in Berlin for the celebrated producer Max Reinhardt. Handsome, dapper and skilled, Ordynski also spoke of the indigenous. "My purpose in settling down in America for a while," he said in January 1915, just before he left Europe for the duration of the war, "is to play a part in the development of the coming American drama. A young, fresh country like the United States ought to create its own particular drama."[13]

Geddes found Miss Barnsdall modest, generous, impatient with details and lacking both in administrative ability and humor. Not long after he got married in March 1916 and gave more style to his name, Bel Geddes traveled to Chicago to meet her again. Then came his introduction to Wright:

Mr. Wright looked kindly and important. He showed us

---

[11] Charles Wakefield Cadman, "The 'Idealization' of Indian Music," *Musical Quarterly*, July 1915, p. 388. Cadman (1881–1946) was among the founders of the Hollywood Bowl; he spent his later years in Los Angeles.

[12] Norman Bel Geddes, *Miracle in the Evening* (New York, 1960), p. 152; subsequent extracts are from pp. 152, 155 and 157. Bel Geddes (1893–1958) designed more than 200 theatrical productions, and was equally successful as an industrial designer. See his *Horizons* (Boston, 1932; Dover reprint, New York, 1977). He also did magazine illustrations for Henry Blackman Sell.

[13] *New York Times*, Jan. 12, 1915, p. 9. Ordynski (1878–1953) was a professor of literature in Poland before he joined Max Reinhardt. In 1917, after a four-week stint as a movie actor, he expressed his ideas about the corrupting demand for "action" in motion pictures; *see* "Action—Camera!," *Theatre Magazine*, Dec. 1917, p. 407. Ordynski returned to Poland in 1920.

around his office which was well filled with objects of art from Japan. He spoke at length about his hotel in Tokyo, saying that it would be his greatest monument. And he spoke very warmly of the Japanese people. It was some time before he mentioned Miss Barnsdall's theater or house . . .

Mr. Wright would have impressed me far more had he not dressed like Elbert Hubbard, and had he not talked like a preacher. What made him want to appear Bohemian? He was the first man I had ever met who looked the way artists were always pictured. He could have walked on stage in *La Bohème* without changing clothes . . . His personality and conversation had a grand and romantic flavor. Most interestingly and almost without pause, he expounded his theories on philosophy, art, morals, and other architects. He appeared to be more intelligent than instinctive artistically, more ingenious than inspirational, and he discussed his work as though Aline and I could not understand even the rudiments. "I prefer to answer questions before they are asked," he would say. His enthusiasm was exciting in itself. It swept him along and us, too. Sometimes he forgot what he was talking about, but he kept right on with something else, and all of it was stimulating.

Wright showed them drawings for Miss Barnsdall's house as well as her theater, Bel Geddes recalled, and to his eyes the house looked highly original but more like a miniature palace from some ancient civilization than a contemporary private home. Sometimes, after the passage of 40 years, Bel Geddes got confused in chronology; but his memory of seeing drawings as early as 1916 for what became Hollyhock House in 1920–21 finds support in the remembrances of Antonin Raymond. Not much was under way at Taliesin when he went to work there in 1916, said Raymond, but "some early sketches" were made for the Barnsdall house.[14] Wright wanted to hold a client's interest, even if that meant sketching a project long before any site was secured—in apparent violation of the idea that the spirit of the landscape ought to figure large in the conception of the house. Miss Barnsdall found it difficult to grasp Wright's imagination, and she very much liked to see perspective drawings or even models. ("I want awfully to see a 'picture' of the hill," she wrote Wright in September 1920, when she hoped to develop the site in Los Angeles with all sorts of buildings. In response, Lloyd Wright went to work on some splendid wash drawings.)

Where would she build the new theater? Wright at first thought it was to be in Chicago, but Miss Barnsdall soon headed West. Her company's version of *Alice in Wonderland*, as dramatized by the Chicago writer Alice Gerstenberg, prompted a review in New York that noted an evident amateurism—a judgment that may have helped turn her westward.[15] For a moment, San Francisco seemed the place. In the summer of 1916 she was already planning a season there, and on July 27 she wrote Wright a breathless letter from Mill Valley:

> Do work on the theatre plans and get them finished as soon as possible for this is the psychological moment and if I do not grip it and build a theatre within the next six months somebody else will. We are looking for land now and I am only waiting for father's very definite consent, he writes constantly that I must wait and have my own theatre, to give out a statement that it is to be built. It must be along the lines of the studio plan and can you tell me roughly what size the lot must be? I want to get the land within the next two months, if possible, and I think it is, so that you may see it when you come out and have the time to build to the best advantage on it.

> You will put your freest dreams into it, won't you! For I believe so firmly in your genius that I want to make it the keynote of my work . . . Things done in the theatre will always have a certain lightness, piquancy and grace, so it should have lovely golds that take the sun!

> Can you give me a rough idea of cost and what is expected of me and when? It must not be a large theatre, not over a thousand, but exquisitely perfect in detail. You can't build a model until you see the site can you? Please let me know all these details. I'm so eager!

But within a few weeks she was caught up in producing her theater season in Los Angeles instead. *Thunderbird* had to be abandoned, Bel Geddes recalled, because hardly anyone in the company could appear credibly as an Indian. Ordynski soon traveled back to New York just to engage more players; California was not yet home to many legitimate actors and actresses.[16] After several weeks of dispiriting rehearsal, Miss Barnsdall also abandoned the production of *Macaire*. Wright wrote her on October 27 that he had heard from his son Lloyd about her pluck in canceling the play before opening night:

> He informed me also that the theatre prospect looked too big to you . . . you know you can borrow 50% of the cost of building and ground together, anywhere, even here. Say you could have $75,000 in cash—and put it into ground that could be valued at $100,000 and if you proposed to improve the ground with a rental-yielding

---

[14] *Antonin Raymond: An Autobiography* (Rutland, Vt., and Tokyo, 1973), p. 53.

[15] *New York Times*, March 24, 1915, p. 11.
[16] *New York Times*, Sept. 27, 1916, p. 9.

building—costing another $100,000—you could borrow $\frac{1}{2}$ or perhaps a little more than $\frac{1}{2}$ of $200,000, or the $100,000 necessary to erect your building.

On a lesser scale the same proportion would hold. If you could determine what sum would be available to work with, I could tell you what the possibilities were and I would work with you on any reasonable plan you might suggest. I have talked about the theatre with no one since I talked with you. . . .

Bel Geddes recalled that Miss Barnsdall would not even show any drawings of the theater to Ordynski, despite his stage expertise and the fact they had become lovers. The first and last season of the Los Angeles Little Theater opened October 31 with *Nju*, directed by Ordynski, before an audience that sparkled with lights from the infant movie colony: Charlie Chaplin, Theda Bara, Douglas Fairbanks, Gloria Swanson, Harold Lloyd, Francis X. Bushman, D. W. Griffith and others. The play was well received. With three more productions and two plays presented especially for children at Christmas time, Miss Barnsdall sustained her season into January 1917.

But the early weeks of the new year grew more difficult. *Everyman*, the final production, was a medieval morality play that Bel Geddes remembered as neither successful nor in any way relevant to Miss Barnsdall's ambitions for the American stage. Miss Barnsdall was pregnant. Ordynski departed for New York, where he soon became stage director for the Metropolitan Opera Company. When he looked back so many years later, Bel Geddes wrote that Miss Barnsdall might have developed the greatest creative theater organization in American history. In 1917, however, that was hardly an opinion shared by Kirah Markham, who had just married Lloyd Wright. In a long letter of February 7 to her father-in-law in Japan, she mentioned an outing the previous day:

Aline Barnsdall was here yesterday. We were motoring together all afternoon and managed fairly well to avoid all mention of the past season and its hardships, but when we got back again to the house, where she had never been excepting to apologize to me for some brutality of mismanagement, it all started again. She really has no actual conception of what she wants to do with a theatre at all. She has vague illuminated moments, but the flashes that come in them are eternally slipping away on close contact with the people she puts in power to execute them . . . And she wants so much to go on. Yet I scarcely believe I could endure the strain of a second season with her. I worked so hard and yet was buffeted all the time by the personal strain between her and the director—who did not like me—that I seem to have

accomplished almost nothing . . . The season is like a bad dream lurking in the back of my mind all the time.

Three weeks later, on February 27, Miss Barnsdall's father died. T. N. Barnsdall left a will written in pen and ink dated 1910. It created a trust of $150,000 to provide monthly income for his sister and six other persons. The remainder of the estate was left in equal shares to Aline and her younger sister Frances, who with her husband Robert Law lived at the home on North Negley Avenue in Pittsburgh. T. N. Barnsdall's estate was appraised at $12,889,435.[17]

In May 1917, Wright returned from Tokyo, where he was working on the Imperial Hotel.[18] Miss Barnsdall moved for a time just north of Seattle, where her child, Aline Elizabeth, was born on August 19.[19] She called her daughter Sugartop—S. T., Sugar Top or simply Sugar—until the girl began to use her middle name, as had her mother and grandmother, and became known as Betty Barnsdall. The child soon gained the distinction of sitting for portraits by two major figures in the history of photography, Edward Weston and Arnold Genthe. However, her mother never knew quite what to do with her. At 35, Miss Barnsdall had remained innocent of any obligation beyond that of entertaining herself. ("I can always create my own little world, for hours at a time, with books, paintings & music," she wrote Wright as late as 1943.) She did feel a certain duty to the stage, Bel Geddes wrote, because the great actress Eleonora Duse had once advised her in the kindest way possible that her gifts resided not in acting but in being able to judge plays—and, given her resources, in being able to produce them.

At first Miss Barnsdall stayed in Seattle with Sugartop. But she was not one to be tied down; for the Christmas holidays, she was off to a ranch in Scottsdale, Arizona. Wright was evidently short of money, as usual, and she sent him a retainer on January 4, 1918:

I enclose a check for $2,500 and some bad news. I won't be able to build this year, not until debts are paid on the estate. Later, I will write you at length. When will your time be in demand on the Tokio hotel and how soon will

---

[17] The will, filed March 5, 1917, is in book 141, No. 168, p. 269 at the Registry of Wills, Allegheny County Court of Common Pleas, Pittsburgh; the inventory and appraisal was filed June 20, 1918, as document No. 65-174-252. Louisa Angela Barnsdall died May 14, 1907, at the age of 53.

[18] For a detailed chronology of Wright's trips to Japan, see Kathryn Smith, "Frank Lloyd Wright and the Imperial Hotel: A Postscript," *Art Bulletin*, June 1985, pp. 296–310.

[19] Ordynski is usually assumed to have been her father, although the birth certificate gives the name of Roy McCheyne George, a writer and longtime friend of Miss Barnsdall's who had a ranch near Phoenix, Arizona. In later years, Miss Barnsdall's daughter maintained that George and her mother had once been married. The family album, now in the Hollyhock House archives, includes pictures of Ordynski from as late as 1925, one of which he inscribed: "To my darling Sugar-Top." In a letter of March 1941 to Wright, Miss Barnsdall writes of her pacifist convictions and adds, "I never felt more passionately about anything excepting Ordynski."

you be free? I probably won't be ready for a year, but when I do, it can be done quickly. I want to start spring of 1919, but can *you?* Everything seems so vague, designs, etc.

The theater remained vague. Her house would come first, she wrote Wright from Seattle on May 30:

I can't say anything more definite about the theatre at present—not until the estate is settled—then I am going to build it as soon as I can. You say you need time to work at it so go ahead, and please have the plans in such form so that we can go over them when I'm in Chicago the *last of June* & take them with me to go over again & again until I *get* your idea of the new forces of interior—in *relation* to the work to be done in it. I will know when it can be built at the end of the summer. The house I can build in the fall, if its cost is not over $25,000. You say "if you are in earnest." I think I've proved that by holding to the idea for so long. How can I *be* with no *real* money behind me just at present!

The baby is a problem. She must have her chance—to grow up into a strong, happy, fullminded young woman. This climate agrees with her—it's wonderful how strong & rosy she is growing—I may have to begin here instead of L.A. It makes no difference—"a thing of beauty is a joy anywhere." Seattle is virgin soil not spoilt by "art movements." I am chafing here. I want to get the estate settled & started but they won't be ready before the last of June. Don't act afraid to let me have the plans. I won't let anybody see them if you don't wish it.

Wright was due to sail again for Japan at the end of October 1918; Miss Barnsdall wrote on October 6 that she hoped to meet him in Los Angeles before he left:

If I don't see you there I will give you a letter to my lawyer, and between you, you may be able to get permission to build, especially as I won't take the ranch if I can't build and the owner is a banker & should have some influence.

I wonder if you would find me a nice rug for my living room, while you are in Japan? I want all the living room & small alcove in light natural wood, much as your own house is—and much the same quality of light and color—like sunshine on a late autumn afternoon—a pale rug, if you understand. I can't pay more than three thousand for it. Then I don't want pictures on my walls in ridiculous frames, but I have two or three that I love—a T.-Lautrec pastel, a Corot and a snow scene by some unknown Norwegian—these I should like built into the walls, just to have a home with some of the

unity of the out of doors. I can live as stuffily as I wish in New York.

Many years later, Miss Barnsdall wrote that she had always loved autumn best. Her feeling for the outdoors and for colors and light must have pleased Wright, but her idea that a few easel paintings could rescue architecture betrayed how poorly she understood his work. Wright had grown to dismiss most representational art as merely sentimental and superfluous. Nor did he intend his architecture to be a simple representation of nature, let alone history. He wanted to control every detail of a design precisely because he meant to make the building a total work of art, as characteristically individual and harmonious as an organism of nature, or as the "unity of the out of doors."

Wright was still in Japan when Miss Barnsdall returned to Los Angeles and at last acquired a building site. She bought an unspoiled hill bordered on the north by Hollywood Boulevard, on the south by Sunset Boulevard, at the east by Vermont Avenue and at the west by Edgemont Street [7]. Once part of the vast Los Feliz ranch, the hill came to be described as lots 40 and 49 of the west portion of the Lick Tract, in the revised plat of Prospect Park. Clearly enough, it was intended to be a square of 40 acres, or a quarter of a quarter-section, a standard parcel of rural land. But the acreage was reduced by the streets and the loss from the northeast corner to the Los Angeles–Pacific Railroad for a curved right-of-way expressed by the street pattern even today. Because the hill was planted with olive trees before the turn of the century, back when Vermont Avenue was called Main Street and Hollywood Boulevard was merely Prospect Avenue, it was known as Olive Hill. Although the hill is often said to comprise 36 acres, various topographical surveys indicate that it comes closer to 35.

Miss Barnsdall bought Olive Hill on June 23, 1919, from Mary Harrison Spires, a widow.[20] After so much secrecy about her plans for a theater, she now became almost effusive. She spoke with a writer for the *Los Angeles Examiner,* and the newspaper concocted a crude cartoon of how Olive Hill might someday look as an "art-theater garden." The paper also asserted that Miss Barnsdall's envisioned producing center might well turn southern California into the acknowledged home of the artistic theater:

The upper story will be made into a roof garden . . . Frank Lloyd Wright, who is to build this theater, now is in Japan . . . It is probable he will return early in September to complete the details of the building, and work will be begun early next year . . .

---

[20] The deed was recorded June 30, 1919, and is filed as Document 163, Deed Book 6870, p. 187 at the Los Angeles County Recorder's Office.

7. Olive Hill in the 1920s, looking northeast.

Her own residence is to surmount the hill . . . "Mr. Wright believes that a California house should be half house and half garden," said she, "and I am strongly of the same opinion. I, therefore, require much room for my own house, but I propose to keep my gardens always open to the public."[21]

The plans for the hill represented a venture she felt compelled to undertake for the sake of ideals, Miss Barnsdall said, for she would rather "vagabond" about the world, amusing herself with her friends, her studies and her love for the out-of-doors. As to the style of the buildings, she responded: "Why not leave that all to the individual judgment of the architect when he sees the land—why shouldn't Mr. Wright evoke a new type of architecture peculiarly fitted to southern California, without borrowing from any other country?"

Between October 1918 and August 1922, Wright made four voyages to Japan and spent less than 12 months on American soil. It was a time of exhausting effort, he recalled, when he was "badgered by increasing domestic infelicity, perplexities and finally the characteristic serious illness that attacks men of the North in that humid Pacific lowland."[22] Miss Barnsdall's mood changed radically between the summer of 1919, when she bought the hill and apparently sailed to Japan to meet with Wright, and the fall of 1921, when the

[21] Florence Lawrence, "Eminence to Be Made Rare Beauty Spot," *Los Angeles Examiner*, July 6, 1919, p. 5.

[22] Wright, *An Autobiography* (1943 edit.), p. 223.

building campaign ceased. A reasonable person might not have found two years an inexcusably long time for the design and construction of a large residence and two lesser houses (as well as the design of other buildings that never got past the drafting table); but Miss Barnsdall did. She began to express anxiety as soon as Wright returned to America. "I so need to get away—new countries always freshen my mind & renew me," she wrote Wright on September 24, 1919, from San Francisco, where she was trying to book passage as far as Australia and Samoa. "If I can't do this I'll come East the middle of October and go over anything with you." Sugar-top, two years old, would stay at Roy George's ranch in Arizona, she said, where "there was an apartment especially built for her that she has never used." Miss Barnsdall was particularly worried about the theater project:

> I had to get away to think and then it was very clear to me that to have a new model made in Japan was extravagant of money & time. I *can't wait*. If I have to wait much longer I'll give it up. I will pay for the model and use it to get the idea & for exhibition purposes— Why two models when every five hundred dollars means so much? The man said he could construct it from plans, and with your help in December he can have it finished before you leave [again for Japan]. As this was the projection of an idea as well as a building, I considered the model as a part of the "preliminaries" and I could not accept or reject the idea until I had seen the model. If the new model is started by the end of October it will be finished by the end of December and I can have it with me for a month or six weeks before I sail.

She shrewdly proposed several changes in the contract that her business manager, Clarence Thomas, had prepared for Wright's services. She also mentioned the possibility of adding a bank building near the apartments she planned along Hollywood Boulevard. And she suggested changes to the theater, about which she reverted to secrecy:

> And *please* let's not talk or show the plans—Let it be seen brilliantly completed. I think it would be a good thing to have an illustrated souvenir, with an article by you, for the opening—and an outline on the program. I also want a place to dance, for I've thought of a way to pay for my experiment, in giving the designer the chance to direct and handle his entire production. Could you possibly get 500 seats for the rehearsal theatre? Perhaps the banquet hall might be turned into a dancing hall and a small library where my apartment was to be. I would rather the young actress and designer should prove themselves in the experimental theatre before going into the larger theatre downstairs.

> Will you write me an exposition of your *organic* idea with illustrations of its practical expression—these can later be incorporated into a book to be sold at the theatre—if you don't object.

> I don't know what I'm going to do about Sugar Top. I don't do anything but feel responsible, hence worry about the socks, ankles and sniffly colds when I'm with her. I'm good for nothing. The minute I get away I forget her existence & think of nothing but the theatre. The delays fill me with forebodings.

> I'm sending you the "notes" on the house in about ten days. The colors I enclose. I expect to be at Taliesin by the last of October—I think the other chance [of the voyage] is so slight.

In a few days, Thomas paid Wright the balance of his fee for preliminary sketches of the house, now expected to cost twice the budget Miss Barnsdall had set only the year before. Thomas also wrote that he would be managing the building fund and would need receipts from Wright to keep a thorough accounting. He soon mailed the revised contract. Miss Barnsdall did not cross the Pacific; she returned instead to Los Angeles, where she grew anxious to see detailed drawings. Every few weeks she sent Wright another telegram, but he continued to live as if by the maxim of Vauvenargues: "To execute great things one must live as though one were never going to die." Life that fall at Taliesin was described many years later by Pauline Schindler, the wife of one of Wright's assistants:

> At ten o'clock in the morning Mr. Wright would come into the studio from his apartment, and the draftsmen would gather around him as he quietly contemplated the work in hand . . . Although the projects were of magnitude, and for weeks at a time the staff might be small, the mood at Taliesin was unhurried . . . Just off the studio in a weather-controlled room were the Japanese prints. An invitation to contemplate them would involve an hour or two of preparation by Mr. Wright and his faithful man Friday, Will Smith, to arrange the exact balanced sequence . . . Will Smith brought to Taliesin its only note of formality. Mr. Wright had both informality and natural grace. Shirts of soft ivory China silk, full-sleeved to the cuff. A suit of soft brown corduroy . . . .[23]

---

[23] "Late Pauline Schindler on Taliesin, 1919," *L.A. Architect*, June 1977, n.p. In an undated letter to Pauline Schindler from Tokyo, probably about 1921, Wright teased her about her apology for an inadvertent "small matter," and candidly described Taliesin: "My situation at Taliesin is at the mercy of the small inadvertencies—with its mixture of sycophants,—servants, students, and illegal friend, with a touch of sincerity here and there thrown in."

Miss Barnsdall traveled to Taliesin twice and was dismayed to find little progress. She also knew that Wright was planning to sail again for Japan in December 1919. She wrote him to say she was turning over to Clarence Thomas all further negotiations: " . . . it is simpler for you & him to discuss the interpretation of the contract—than for you & me. We have something too wonderful to get done to waste time—or jeopardize it in discussion."

Wright telegraphed her on December 9 that his son Lloyd had left Chicago for Los Angeles two days before, and that all was ready for estimates and landscaping. He suggested that they meet him in Seattle before he set sail on December 16. "Do not let this disconcert our work," he said. "All will finally go well." A few days later, Lloyd Wright wrote a long letter to his father:

Saw Aline Barnsdall yesterday. Settled the matter of salary and cost limit for the building and first unit of construction. Have gotten in touch with three contractors so far and am lining up others . . . Miss Barnsdall cannot make the trip to Portland [sic] or does not want to. It seemed to me best to stay here. Keep on the job and attention riveted to it for moral effect if nothing else. Little we could do together in a day at most.

She feels that you are neglecting her interests shamefully, but seems to be pretty game about it, I must confess. As I look at things developing I do not wonder that you are always in confusion and that you cannot accomplish matters in a clean straightforward way. A little rotten luck mixed in with evasion, suspicion and indifference can work "Hell."

The day I arrived I met Robertson, a young contractor here doing government and general business building construction. I knew him in San Diego and Los Angeles. It seems he is connected with a two million dollar venture here and they are looking for an architect. He asked me if I would have you meet his people. I will do what I can and report. But if you wonder why it is you do not get work in this country, here is the answer. You're not here to get it. But cheer up—we will do the best we can and better than we have ever done before. Whether that will be good enough under the circumstances remains to be seen.

This is important. Will you send on your sketch plans so that the model of the theater may proceed and Miss Barnsdall is kept busy playing with it until you get back in the spring. I don't think it will do any harm, and it certainly will keep her mind off the first unit [Hollyhock House] while construction is going on . . .

You are having a model made up in Japan that will be correct. Do you think it would be all right to have this temporary toy setup for her? She needs some concrete object to tie her mind to . . . .

Lloyd Wright at 29 had traveled in Europe and worked on both coasts, usually as a landscape architect. He was confident he could give Hollyhock House a fair start. "I will pull this end thru to some sort of a satisfactory conclusion," he wrote his father in December 1919. "Will probably have construction at a critical point about May or June."

DELAYS AND DISTRESS

WRIGHT KEPT PRETENDING during the fall of 1919 that the drawings for Hollyhock House were much further along. In truth, they could not suffice for construction bids; Lloyd Wright wrote from Los Angeles that he would hire a draftsman for a few weeks or a month just for that purpose. Other drawings in need of more detail, he told his father, would be mailed to R. M. Schindler, one of the few assistants left at Taliesin. "All matters of design," he wrote, "will be referred back to Schindler and yourself before actual construction commences."

How much of the house did Wright imagine before Miss Barnsdall bought the site? His early sketches and perspective studies lack dates; some renderings, fairly precise, could have preceded the rough sketches he made of Olive Hill with various buildings spaced among the trees [8]. These brisk studies of the hill show how much easier it is to handle nature architecturally than to create an architecture naturally. The trees at the top can be grouped into a silhouette like that of the proposed theater. (Later, they would be parted at angles like those in the upper walls of Hollyhock House.) The middle sketch is the most important, not because it depicts the theater on Vermont Avenue, but because Wright labels it the "Front on Minor Axis." This means that although the hill is virtually square, he has chosen an east–west line as the major axis, and the longer fronts of the house will be those on the south and north. He nevertheless ponders the minor axis in three studies for the west front [9–11].

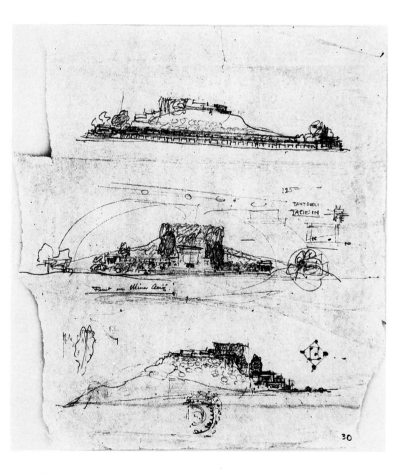

8. Elevation sketches of Olive Hill (from top): north face on Hollywood Boulevard; east face on Vermont Avenue; south face on Sunset Boulevard.

9. Study of west front with hip roofs.

10. Study of west front with pyramidal roofs.

In this brilliant sequence of drawings, Wright breaks from his prairie idiom to invent a new architecture for a much different climate and way of life. Neither the plan nor the massing can dictate to his level of imagination the final appearance of the house: The basic arrangement stays the same, but he proceeds from a house with a family of hip roofs to one in which the roofs are not even visible. The final study thus represents a great turning point in his career. No wonder that in his autobiography he compares the house to his own home in Wisconsin, and writes that "Hollyhock house was to be a natural house, naturally built; native to the region of California as the house in the Middle West had been native to the Middle West."[1]

Now the house has its identity, although not all its details. Still to be developed are the entrance loggia, animal pens, garage, terraces, child's room, living room and the entire ornamental scheme [12–16]. The extraordinary wealth of studies for Hollyhock House merely excited Miss Barnsdall to ask for even more pictures of both the inside and out. "I did not lose my head!" she exclaimed, in beginning a letter of January 7, 1920:

When you were in Los Angeles last fall, you told me that if I would come on to Taliesin the last of October, that you would have for me "Interior Elevations" and "drawings" of the general composition of the hill "in color." Dozens of them—was how you put it.

We were to go over them there at our leisure, and decide. I came. They weren't ready. Because Raymond had not arrived—you explained. I went to New York, and returned a month later; still they were not ready. Raymond had just arrived, and I then expected to see them in Los Angeles.

I am only asking for what you have already promised and what we cannot go on, without. It isn't practical.

So I am writing you just what I expect.

The house must be finished—but if you find it impossible to continue with the theatre in the only way that is safe for me,—we must decide to give it up. Though I earnestly hope this will not be necessary . . .. We won't argue further—only give it up as too gigantic an undertaking.

This is what I expect: "colored elevations" of the living-room group, music room and hall.

---

[1] Wright, *An Autobiography*, p. 227. A. N. Rebori, in "Frank Lloyd Wright's Textile-Block Slab Construction," *Architectural Record*, December 1927, p. 451, noted that in Hollyhock House "the hat of the early type is removed for a flat roof." Wright's first California house, for George C. Stewart in Montecito, was similar to his Middle West work.

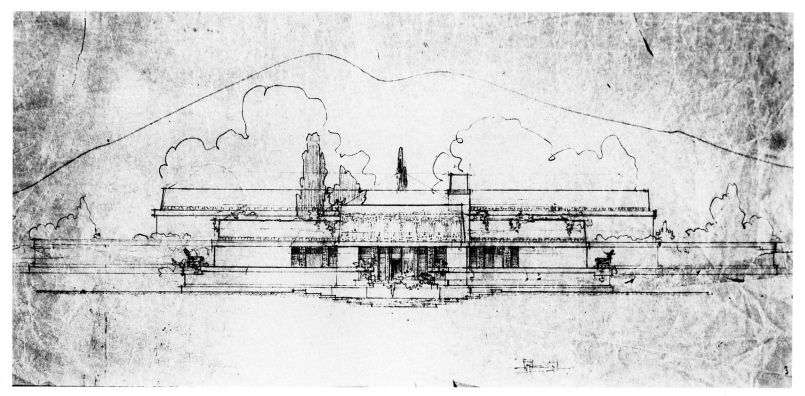

11. Study of west front with flat roofs and pitched upper walls.

OPPOSITE, TOP: 12. Perspective study of west front. OPPOSITE, BOTTOM: 13. Aerial perspective study with terrace in front of living room. ABOVE: 14. Aerial perspective study with terraces at sides of living room.

15. Perspective study of west front, with profusion of hollyhocks.

This section was to have a wood treatment of untouched walnut—combined with the soft purple I showed you in your Japanese prints,—and a touch of gold to link it with the [Japanese] screens. You will remember there will be screens along the two big expanses of wall,—built in,—so the woodwork may be designed to meet them. That will leave very little woodwork in the living room.

In the music room,—the low partition between the music room and the hall, and the side wall of the music room with the Monet built into the design, will be of the wood . . .. I don't care whether or not the plaster peeps through a design of woodwork in places,—but I want the *feeling to be of wood*.

The dining room—wainscoting,—if you wish to call it that—but it is up to your imagination to make it something else . . .. All I want is a mahogany background for my mahogany table, golden rug, and curtains.

The other elevations need not be in color, as they must blend with the furniture I already have. These rooms will be plaster and wood trimmings of course, and I don't think you can do much until you see the furniture.

The house can easily be finished . . .. It is too large, but necessarily so for its position. It is absolutely beautiful in architecture and I feel that you did work with me in spirit in designing it . . ..

I am going to Europe the last of this month to be gone

until spring,—or until you have started across the Pacific—don't come . . . unless everything is completed,—for it will only waste our time.

I am going to let Lloyd proceed as planned, because S.T. needs her home so badly. Will allow for woodwork as desired. If it comes beyond the prescribed sum, we will shorten the pergola screen [animal pens] connecting with the garage, and cut off the bay window in the rear. I hope we won't have to, for I see the architectural necessity of it.

I won't have the house cheapened in quality,—for if it is, the theatre might as well not be built.

Like many people with little to do, Miss Barnsdall was always in a rush. She thought she knew her mind but she changed it frequently. In another letter that month, she told Wright it was a pity he was not in Los Angeles. Although their relations were strained, in a sense she was right. ("Where I am my office is," Wright wrote in an angry letter of June 1931 to Schindler. "My office is *me*. Frank Lloyd Wright has no other office, never had one and never will have one.") Miss Barnsdall went on:

Now please do as wonderful a thing with the inside of my house as . . . with the outside. The designs Lloyd gave me from your specifications looked as though you

16. Study of south front.

had thought very little about them—they lacked ingenuity and care of the outside handling. We are going ahead with it but worry because you are not here to decide on the color. I don't want it to *look* green but to *feel* green as a background for the rich hollyhock and rose reds . . . .

I suppose Lloyd has written you that we have taken out the two bedrooms on the second floor over the servants' quarters and put in one large one for me. I want to sleep in the center of the hill, away from the outer fringe of noise and next to the Hollywood Hills. The other room will not be changed but done in hollyhock and green as planned . . . I want the house just as it is with the bay window at the back even if it does mean a few thousand more because I see the architectural necessity of the bay window . . . .

Please, please have things visualized for me by spring even to rugs and furniture for I want to work like blazes when you return . . . I am in bed this moment with a bad cold. I am just restlessly wearing myself out with waiting . . . .

Lloyd Wright could not foresee that Schindler would take so long with the working drawings, or that after his father returned to Taliesin the drawings would be revised even into August and September [17–21]. There was little he could do but prepare the site and begin the landscaping, as he wrote his father on March 22, 1920:

I am enclosing two letters recently sent Schindler. It took the first one to make him disgorge the plans which I now have in hand. Possibly I have been hyper-critical. I don't enjoy forcing a man's hand, but it seemed in this case and so far as I could manage it, the only way in which I could get results . . .

Miss B. is anxious to get the house under way and the walls up ready for your finishing hand in May . . . Am forwarding photos of the work on the models [of the theater] and the hill planting. Also Schindler's plans for the house as far as he has gone . . . Miss B. waits in New York for your return . . . .

Hollyhock House evidently was conceived as a structure in reinforced concrete, and is often mistaken to be. Curiously, none of the working drawings show it as such. Even before the specifications were revised in March 1920 they called for bearing walls of hollow terra-cotta tile, with the faces well scored to receive a stucco finish. The upper walls were to be of stucco over wood framing, and were to rest on a concrete beltcourse [22]. Many years later, Miss Barnsdall was concerned about repairs to Hollyhock House and to

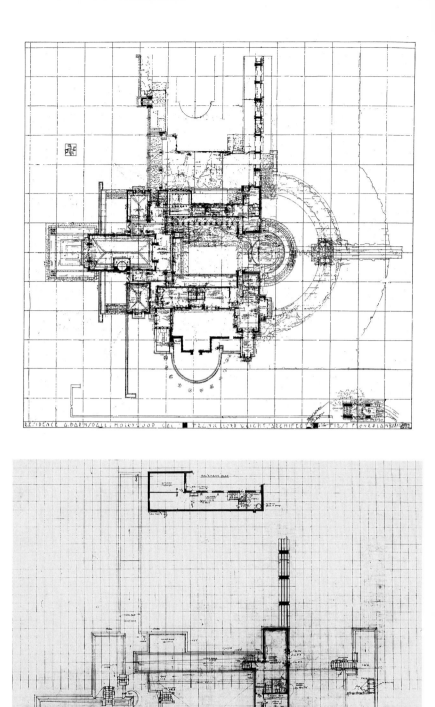

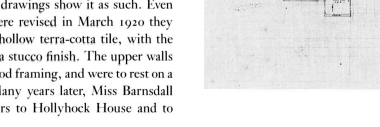

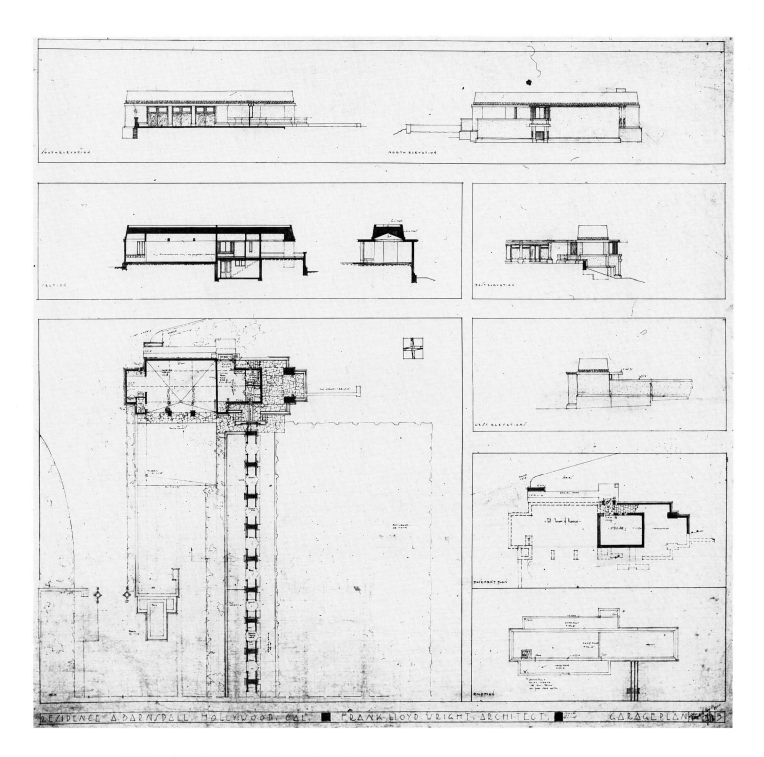

RESIDENCE A BARNSDALL, HOLLYWOOD, CAL. ■ FRANK LLOYD WRIGHT, ARCHITECT, ■ GARAGE PLAN

OPPOSITE, TOP: 17. First-floor plan on twenty-foot grid, revised September 1920. OPPOSITE, BOTTOM: 18. Plan of second floor and roofs on four-foot grid, revised September 1920. ABOVE: 19. Garage plans, elevations and sections.

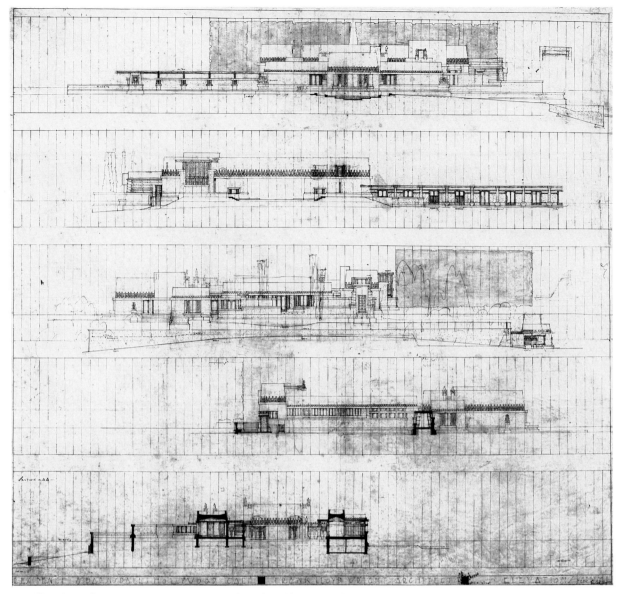

20. Elevations: (from top) west, east, south and north; with section through garden court, looking west.

Residence "B," a subsidiary house down the west slope of Olive Hill. "The walls were a cheap substitute for proper earthquake construction," Wright wrote her on May 28, 1943. "I am sorry we ever used them." In reinforced concrete, Hollyhock House would have had greater structural integrity. But it would look the same; there is little difference between cement stucco and smooth-finished concrete. Wright in fact had praised cement as a "simplifier, enabling the artist to clothe the structural frame with a simple, modestly beautiful robe."[2] The naked display of structure played no important role in his architecture. Nor, apart from the

danger of earthquakes, did Hollyhock House call for exceptional structure: The only cantilever of significant scale was that of the canopy at the porte-cochere. It was not until 15 years later, as Wright wrote, in the Edgar Kaufmann weekend house above the waterfalls of Bear Run, in southwestern Pennsylvania, that "reenforced concrete was actually needed to construct the cantilever system of this extension of the cliff beside a mountain stream."[3]

Ornament and structure in Hollyhock House thus bear an unusual relation: Although the ornament brings to the house its lilt and grace, it is darker than the stuccoed walls and, indeed, heavier. Art-stone, defined as a mixture of cement with screened granite and gravel, was specified for sills,

[2] *Catalogue of the Fourteenth Annual Exhibition of the Chicago Architectural Club* (Chicago, 1901), n.p. By using stucco, Wright challenged in its own terms the highly popular Spanish Colonial Revival of southern California.

[3] *Architectural Forum*, Jan., 1938, p. 36.

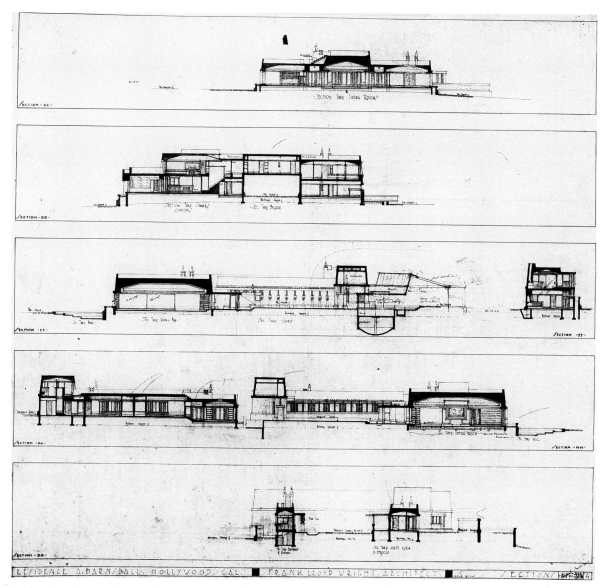

21. Sections (from top): through living room, looking east; owner's quarters and bridge, looking west; living room and court, looking north (with art gallery project at east); owner's quarters, looking north; owner's quarters, guest rooms and library, looking south; court and living room, looking south; kitchen, court, pergola and guest room, looking east.

copings and "all surfaced concrete work, [such] as bases, fireplaces, flower boxes, stone ornaments, capitals, etc." In short, art-stone serves sometimes as ornament and sometimes as structure. Some of the early sketches for the house show no ornamentation, but depict hollyhocks: biennial plants, native to China, that grow six to eight feet tall and have coarse leaves and showy spikes of clustered flowers [23]. "A bit sentimental," Wright wrote later, "Miss Barnsdall had pre-named the house for the Hollyhock she loved for many reasons, all of them good ones, and called upon me to render her favorite flower as a feature of Architecture how I might."[4]

Hollyhocks have alternate leaves, but the abstractions in the house are bilaterally symmetrical. One abstraction com-

4 Wright, *An Autobiography*, p. 226.

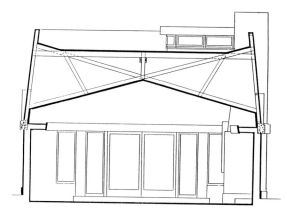

22. Diagram of living-room structure; heavy lines indicate finished surfaces. Wood trusses rest on concrete beltcourse, which caps lower walls of hollow clay tile.

ABOVE: 23. Hollyhocks at south front. RIGHT: 24. South living-room door, with hollyhock column and hollyhock frieze. (Ezra Stoller © Esto) OPPOSITE, LEFT: 25. Hollyhock finial at roof; note glyphlike motif at top. OPPOSITE, RIGHT: 26. Hollyhock flower urn by south living-room terrace. (Ezra Stoller © Esto)

poses the frieze around the living room and second story; another adorns the principal posts of the living room, alcoves and loggia [24]. A different motif, elaborated from the pitch in the upper walls, serves in a secondary frieze for the lesser rooms—the music room, library, dining room, guest rooms and kitchen—and for the garage. In a variant and expanded form, it enriches the sides of the subordinate posts of the living room and loggia, and the posts in the music room, library and hall [see 65]. It also can be found inverted in the short posts of the west wall of the entrance loggia [see 57]. A different abstraction (or "formalized hollyhock," as Miss Barnsdall called it) appears in the capitals of the colonnade near the water garden [see 112–116]. Still another forms the sloped finials that rise with such vigor from the roof [25]. A hollyhock abstraction in embryo can be discovered in the canted posts at the east wall of the entrance loggia. Paired hollyhock abstractions support the flower urns that stand as terminals to the terrace walls, as well as a double-sized urn,

more than nine feet long, near the service entrance. The urns have sloped sides, which again answer to the pitch of the upper walls [26].

The hollyhock ornaments of the primary frieze stand 38 inches tall; those on the primary posts rise 54 inches. By no means are they incidental details. Through a lively inventiveness and mastery of scale, the ornamentation manifests the spirit of the house. A critic who faulted what he described as "the exuberance of the inappropriate ornament" drew a sharp reply from Wright. "The Barnsdall house ornament," Wright wrote, "is as appropriate as the house itself. If the house is inappropriate then the ornament is so."[5]

---

[5] Letter of Feb. 26, 1932, to Henry-Russell Hitchcock, in Wright, *Letters to Architects*, ed. Bruce Brooks Pfeiffer (Fresno, Calif., 1984), p. 135. Hitchcock's comments on Hollyhock House appeared in the Museum of Modern Art exhibition catalogue, *Modern Architecture* (New York, 1932), pp. 34–35. He wrote that after Wright's experience in Japan the California climate reinforced the "intoxication of a foreign land." The ornament of the house is in fact as judicious as it is inventive.

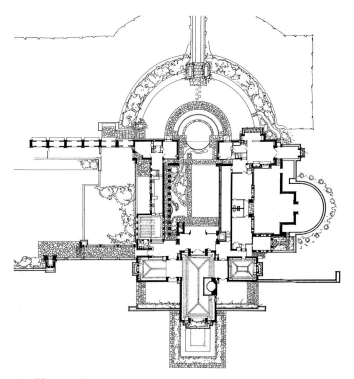

27. Plan as redrawn and rotated.

The ornamentation proves as constitutional as the plan is ornamental: a fact made clear when the plan was redrawn for publication and cunningly rotated to display better its abstract graphic power and kinship with the hollyhock abstractions [27]. Superimposed squares and rectangles visually weight the base of the typical hollyhock ornament; in the plan, the reiterated squares of the reflecting pool join the rectangle of the living room (itself a double square). The hollyhock ornament rises with parallel stems, and the plan culminates in a long eastward path defined by parallel flowered borders. In this process of high abstraction, Hollyhock House achieves an integrity of form far more characteristic and purposeful than that of a house planned simply to satisfy the usual values of shelter and comfort. It emulates nature; in the same way, an organism attains the perfect beauty of an eloquent form beyond simple response to function. Purpose in nature means the fulfillment, or maturity, of a form.[6]

Hollyhock House in May 1920 had fallen so far behind schedule it was in no sense ready for the architect's "finishing hand." Little was accomplished during the entire year. S. G. H. Robertson, whom Lloyd Wright knew from earlier years in San Diego and Los Angeles, seems not to have been ap-

pointed the builder before the end of April, and the permit was not issued until May 19.[7] Miss Barnsdall stayed at Moosehead Lake in Maine and made periodic trips to New York to visit her dentist's office. She grew reluctant to begin the Olive Hill project, as she warned Wright in a letter of May 30:

> Don't you think it is time that we forgot our personal feelings and began to work? The theatre is going to be built—the *group* not costing over $310,000 as planned, and no work is to begin until it has been so completely finished in *drawn* plans that complete specifications can be given to contractors—I won't turn one shovelful of earth until I know the cost of the whole—even to equipment. You can see that we have a lot of work before us.
>
> Don't talk about my treating you badly. You know that I like & admire you as an individual almost more than anyone I know—as an architect, too, or I wouldn't have chosen you—*but*—as a *creator* you would spend my whole fortune to create a perfect thing—it is the nature of creation. Why combat it and pretend something else. And I as the general director of an enterprise can only spend a certain amount . . . We are going to be enemies on those points, but let's be *reasonable* enemies & good friends between times. It's one of the human limitations of the work. I think it will be delightful working out the hill with you, if we are both perfectly direct and understanding. I have the money for the remainder of the hill . . . Now ally yourself with me in this undertaking. I am giving you most—tho' I won't be a slave to anybody's ideas . . . I cannot believe with the belief of the creator but with the belief of the critic. This angers & discourages every artist at first, but they remain my friends after it is over because they know it isn't just blind worship that I give . . .
>
> Lloyd has probably told you that I lost my passport three days before I was to sail [for Europe] because of my friendship for Emma Goldman . . . .

Anarchist, pacifist, feminist, social revolutionist and tireless agitator, Emma Goldman had been imprisoned for conspiring against the draft. In December 1919, a few months after her release, she and her longtime associate Alexander Berkman, who in 1892 had tried to assassinate Henry Clay Frick, were deported to Russia. Miss Barnsdall "appeared to have made a present of $2,500 to Emma Goldman at the time

---

[6] See the *Physics*, sec. 199a, in *The Basic Works of Aristotle*, ed. Richard McKeon (New York, 1941), p. 250. F. Nietzsche, in *The Birth of Tragedy*, carried this idea further by asserting that "it is only as an *aesthetic phenomenon* that existence and the world are eternally *justified*." See *Basic Writings of Nietzsche*, ed. Walter Kaufmann (New York, 1966), p. 52.

[7] Permits Nos. 7303 and 7304 (the garage), Board of Public Works. The size of the house was stated as 120 by 140 feet—figures derived from the twenty-foot modules of the site plan. *Southwest Builder and Contractor*, May 7, 1920, p. 12, reported that Robertson would "superintend" the project, estimated to cost $50,000.

Goldman and Berkman were deported," according to an intelligence report of March 1922 to J. Edgar Hoover, then assistant director of the Bureau of Investigation. (The agency, renamed the Federal Bureau of Investigation in 1935, continued to enlarge Miss Barnsdall's dossier with stray facts and rumors, most of them downright silly, until the last years of her life.)

Now began the months of what Wright remembered as "friction, waste and slip."[8] Most of the time, he and Miss Barnsdall were far apart and far from Los Angeles. Their representatives could hardly stand to deal with each other. Even the role of S. G. H. Robertson came into question. Was he the general contractor or the superintendent of a special construction company organized for Miss Barnsdall by her business manager, Clarence Thomas? The working drawings also became a point of contention. Wright often used a unit system of measurement—four feet, for Hollyhock House—in place of explicit and accurate dimensions. Drawings that looked sketchy to begin with might soon be revised, or further improvised, as construction proceeded: ". . . we would have to amplify the sketches into plans as best we could, making such added notes and details as we went along as would suffice to get the building properly built."[9]

Thomas was pledged to control costs, but Wright demanded a large margin for changes in the field. Wright's superintendents were neither experienced nor skilled in construction scheduling, or in dealing with suppliers, subcontractors, tradesmen and city officials. If the situation was all too familiar to Wright, it nevertheless was exacerbated by the importance of the house, and the amount of thought he had given it in seeking a new architecture. The wishes of Miss Barnsdall, finally, as to colors and materials, furniture and easel paintings, were bound to conflict with the intense discipline of Wright's design, his drive to achieve a totally harmonious work of art. "All in all," the Viennese architect Richard Neutra wrote his wife in 1924, after his first sight of Wright's work in the Chicago area, "it was no disillusion. However, the people who live in these houses were rather awful. I had always hoped that this new architecture would produce a different human being. I am sorry to be proved wrong."[10] In November 1930, Wright wrote Miss Barnsdall a letter in which he extended affection to his "most difficult client." Perhaps she was.

Hollyhock House in construction exhausted everyone. The account Wright gives in his autobiography, an unusually

long episode, thus unfolds as a lament over the struggle in architecture between imagination and execution. The same parties that make architecture possible—the client and the contractor—too often inhibit or subvert the realization of the work of art. Wright consequently expresses his admiration for the art of music. Although the tone of this episode seems tinged with self-pity, Wright stays scrupulously loyal to fact.

At first, Hollyhock House was impeded by plans for the theater, destined never to be resolved. Miss Barnsdall held back, even after Robertson had begun the foundation work for the house and had approved payment for 4,050 cubic feet of concrete and 21,861 bricks. "Whole group an entity," she wired Wright from New York on July 21. "Would change plan if theater not built and must know cost [of the] group before beginning." She was back in Hollywood by August 5, when she sent another wire. "When am I to expect you? It is better to go over everything on spot. Am reassured as to size [of the theater] but alterations a surprise. Please get here as soon as possible. Can only discuss changes with you." Wright responded that he dreaded another transcontinental trip in the heat. Miss Barnsdall returned to New York. In a letter of September 14 she begged to see a "picture" of the hill; ten days later she asked if he would be ready to meet her by October 1. Wright was busy with such details as a full-scale drawing for the ornamental pattern on the sides of the slender art-stone posts in the living room, library, music room and hall. Other buildings for the hill were also in design, he telegraphed her on September 24:

Impossible to get help—we have been working day and night since I got home—nearly worn out. If you can delay until Oct. 10th to 15th much better. All details for Own House and Residence "A" in Los Angeles. Stores and Small Dwellings and Residence "B" nearing completion. Rug designs and furniture designs ready—but no perspective drawings yet. Experts promised finally to come to work Monday.

Again, he exaggerated. Robertson meantime continued to work at the site. He sunk below the garden court a huge cistern intended to collect the rainwater from the roof terraces. He paid for another 1,471 cubic feet of concrete and for 4,845 hollow tiles of various sizes. Soon, however, the construction process broke down. Miss Barnsdall telegraphed Wright from Los Angeles on October 22, 1920:

Work on house halted. Details for base stone work not ready. Following details are immediately needed: Beam details for patio and hall. Brick openings for doors and windows. Electrical layout. Setting plans for stone. Mill work doors and windows. Glass contracts. Sheet metal work . . . Send furniture and rug designs.

[8] Wright, An Autobiography, pp. 231, 233. The phrase is from a poem by Rudyard Kipling that Wright displayed on the balcony parapet of his Oak Park studio.
[9] Wright, An Autobiography, p. 229.
[10] Richard Neutra, Promise and Fulfillment: 1919–1932, ed. Dione Neutra (Carbondale, Ill., 1986), p. 120.

The electrical contractor, Harris G. Stone, withdrew on November 5. He wrote that he had signed an agreement June 17 to have his work finished by October:

> Over four and one half months have passed . . . and the buildings have not progressed to a stage of completion where I could complete my part of the agreement. Continued effort on my part has failed up to the present date to bring into my hands accurate and sufficiently complete drawings and information necessary for the proper execution of the job.

> In order that you may appreciate why I was attracted to this piece of work, I would say that I saw in it new and original engineering problems which were revolutionary forward and which would use some of my technical training not required in executing the average electrical contract.

Stone offered to remove his unused electrical material, and asked to be paid for what little work he had been able to perform. When he got no answer either from Lloyd Wright or Clarence Thomas, he sent his bill and retained an attorney. His complaint went unanswered until December 16 and unresolved until February 24 of the next year.

Of much greater moment, an ugly incident at the building site made it impossible for Lloyd Wright to continue as the clerk-of-the-works. "I know the reason he left the job," his son Eric Lloyd Wright said not long ago. "The contractor had been pouring one of the pools—I don't know which pool—something was done improperly, and my father got into an argument with the contractor and got the contractor so mad he came rushing after him with an ax. My dad grabbed him and threw him into the pond. After that, my grandfather had Schindler come out, because of course my father couldn't get along with the contractor."[11]

Wright and Schindler arrived in Los Angeles early in December 1920, shortly before Wright was to sail again for Japan. The number of building projects Miss Barnsdall hoped to undertake on Olive Hill only magnified the troubled state of affairs. She had asked Wright to bring with him "everything possible to ensure good generalship" as well as a number of pictorial drawings of the buildings she contemplated: not just the theater, Hollyhock House and the lesser Residences "A" and "B," but terrace shops, apartments, a director's house and a motion-picture theater [28]. She also planned to take control of the faltering construction process.

R. M. Schindler, 33 years old, was an imaginative architect. When he left Vienna in 1914 to accept a post in a large Chicago architectural office, he already knew of Wright's

work through the great portfolio published in Berlin in 1910. "Here was 'space architecture,' " he once wrote. "Here was the first architect." Schindler seemed constitutionally disposed to Wright's art. "The old problems have been solved and the styles are dead," Schindler wrote in a manifesto of 1912. "The architect has finally discovered the medium of his art: SPACE. A new architectural problem has been born."[12] He went to work for Wright early in 1918, and later lived for a time in Wright's former home in Oak Park. Wright considered him inexperienced, paid him almost nothing and enjoyed his company. "Rudy was too smooth ever to learn how to be serious, which was why I liked him," Wright recalled in his autobiography.[13]

Schindler was far from smooth, however, in handling Hollyhock House; he compounded the difficulties he was sent to overcome. His contentiousness no doubt was encouraged by Wright's bad example. Schindler wrote more letters than Miss Barnsdall, and as if he meant to engage in as many skirmishes as possible. He got off to a bad start: not just with the electrical contractor, but with the stonemakers (the William Smith Architectural Concrete Stone Company of Pasadena), with the masonry contractor Robert Preston, with S. G. H. Robertson and with Clarence Thomas. He also caused problems with Residences "A" and "B," which were to be built by a second contractor, C. D. Goldthwaite. Early in January 1921, Lloyd Wright sent a tardy report to his father:

> This is hardly a weekly report. We will call it a beginning. Fell ill the day after you left and was down with a severe case of grip. Half sick during the holiday season, but am now back in the harness strong again.

> The drawing for Miss Barnsdall is of course late but it has turned out beautifully better than the first—am sending a photo of it to you. Schindler frets at the time it consumes, and so it does. But it must be done. He chafes in the harness and has bewailed the fact that you forbade him to get in touch with Miss B. I have not been able to give him much assistance, hardly any in fact, between the landscape work which I am pushing rapidly along and the perspectives and sickness.

> He had considerable difficulty with the building dept. and discovered to his chagrin that the plans he drew up were very sketchy and incomplete. It angers me to see how glibly he places the responsibility for their incompleteness on your shoulders. However, he has had to do the work of bringing them up to snuff, at least suffi-

[11] Conversation of Aug. 30, 1990.

[12] Esther McCoy, *Five California Architects* (New York, 1960), p. 152, and McCoy, in *R. M. Schindler* (Santa Barbara, Calif., 1967), pp. 7–8.
[13] Wright, *An Autobiography*, p. 229.

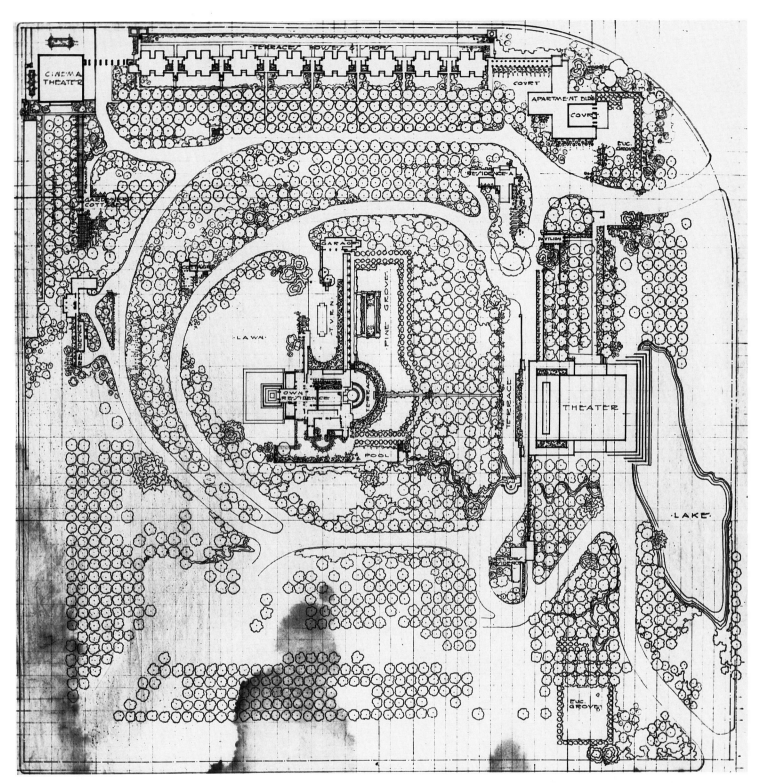

28. General planting plan of Olive Hill.

ciently to pass the building dept. So they—Residences "A" and "B"—are ready for signing up. But as you perhaps do not know, Miss B. has formed a company, a holding construction co. to carry on the work on the Hill. That is, Thomas was supposed to have done so . . .

You may be sure Goldthwaite dug into the new corporation. The first thing he discovered was that it was no corporation at all, and not legal. So he has forced them to incorporate legally before he will do business with them . . .

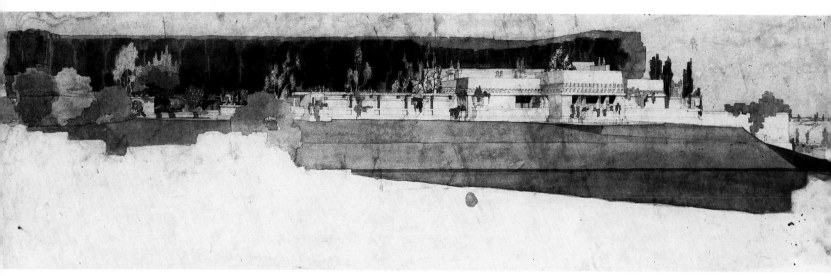

29. Rendering of west front by Lloyd Wright.

30. Aerial perspective by Lloyd Wright.

Fortunately, and strangely enough, Thomas has allowed me to proceed full speed ahead with the landscape work without questions and has signed up contracts in Aline's name. And I'm pushing it while I may.

Rudolph has caught Robertson in a proposition whereby Robertson was going to put over a deal with a plaster contractor. He nipped it in the bud, and Robertson swore at him and said he'd get him. I really didn't think Robertson would give way that easily. But he has quite badly on the job and it is dragging as badly as before. They're all jumping in on Rudolph, but from all indications he is well able to hold his own.

Smith is still kicking, and Preston too, of course . . . Of course it stands to reason that [Robertson] is agitating the subcontractors on the job also to make it as much trouble for the architect as possible. The condition is an intolerable one and must end soon . . . .

Lloyd Wright had moved to an apartment near Olive Hill so that he could be closer to his landscape work. He was also beginning divorce proceedings against Kirah Markham. Schindler began the new year by badgering the William Smith Architectural Concrete Stone Company. He said the roof trusses were being delayed by the slow production of the art-stone sills and posts on which they were to bear. George Taylor replied for the company on January 5. He wrote that the measurements simply were not working out:

In one instance at the music room there is a discrepancy of at least one foot . . . we do not find any attention has been given to the fact that a great deal of stone work must be made to fit *the building;* the unit system of estimating measurements employed by you on this work has proven very costly to us from the very start of this contract, and in order to expedite our work, we delegated one draftsman to devote all of his time . . . He worked several weeks and failed to connect with practical requirements; later we found out that he could make no progress as the general outlines shown on your blueprints show a great lack of attention to necessary detail . . . .

Similar problems plagued Robert Preston, the masonry contractor, who in a letter of February 22 repeated his request that the terms of his agreement be revised:

I will commence with the statement that my contract on the unit basis was entered into and became effective on the 29th day of May 1920, the work involved to be carried on without delay so that the building would be completed speedily. The urgency was so great I was not able to benefit by the prices of the Los Angeles Pressed Brick Company I had used in basing my price for setting the hollow tile . . . Then after all the hurry the tile delivered in June lay on the ground unused for over two months . . . And in regard to the art-stone I had agreed to set, I later discovered the contract for furnishing [it] had not been let, and it was four months before I was able to commence to set any stone . . . .

Preston stated other complaints: the cement he was asked to use with brickwork was not in the specifications, and his masons refused to work with it; no setting plans were provided by the architect; and Lloyd Wright misled him by saying that most of the art-stone members could be handled without a derrick.

Miss Barnsdall had left New York for Europe on January 25, 1921—not without having sent a parting shot at Wright, in Japan:

Tomorrow I am sailing for Europe to stay until my house is completely finished. This will probably be a satisfaction to you because it leaves you the choice of a number [of things] . . .

Everything is now arranged so that the two houses ["A" and "B"] can be built, a certain part of the landscape finished & the roads finished. I can take no further responsibility until my home is *complete* and ready to live in, according to present specifications . . . I can't proceed [with the other large buildings] until my house is finished. It grows too confusing. Sloane's will make the rug.

Not long after Miss Barnsdall left the country, Lloyd Wright sent his father a photograph of one of the wash renderings he had so lovingly made to answer her demand for pictures [29,30]. His vision of the house could make it all seem worthwhile. Lloyd Wright was not fond of Schindler, and he was happy to be supervising the landscaping of the hill rather than the house itself:

The landscape work progresses smoothly. Miss B. has opened the door here generously. Thomas is tending to his knitting. Robertson is about finished, wants to quit I believe . . . Previous to Schindler's coming and the new work, I got along on my salary and less than a hundred a month for office expenses—but the case is different now. There is more work to be done, and work [of] a first class and not indifferent or got by fashion.

We are now alone—no draftsmen—Rudolph and myself and the boy are the office force really good enough for the work-load. The difference between working with a contractor on the job and doing the work oneself is indeed considerably different: no worry or drag and real pressure in the work. It is early yet to prophesy what Goldthwaite will prove to be, but so far it looks promising . . . .

C. D. Goldthwaite had signed a contract on January 14 to build Residences "A" and "B." Almost immediately, Schindler began sending him annoying and critical letters. Schindler nevertheless thought more of Goldthwaite than he did of S. G. H. Robertson (whose initials Schindler seemed to make a point of scrambling—a tactic he probably learned from Wright). Wright and Schindler had agreed that Goldthwaite might make a good replacement for Robertson in building Hollyhock House; but Thomas would hear nothing of it, as he wrote Schindler on March 10:

We will proceed with the building of the dwelling as we have in the past—I am not accepting the suggestion emanating from your office that we turn over the finishing of the building to Mr. Goldthwaite or any other contractor . . .

I am tired of your camouflage. You must think that you are damn wise or I am a damn fool. Try for a time to play with the truth.

There is no politics. That's your excuse. And the hedge behind which you wish to hide—when you are confronted with your own plottings. Enough of this! Do the work you are being paid to do—and the work will proceed as it should.

By the middle of April 1921 the building process had grown still more muddled. The art-stone was not all in place, and the plastering contractor, E. O. Ward, had to postpone the interior work for fear it would be stained as further art-stone members were set. In turn, the millwork from the Weldon & Glasson Planing Mill in San Diego was kept waiting on the plasterer for finished openings. Weldon & Glasson warned that because the measurements of the openings so often were revised, the leaded glass from the Judson Studio, in Los Angeles, should be delayed until the sash was fitted. For months, the colors of the living-room rug were in question, and it was the middle of April before Schindler finally approved the yarn samples.

Miss Barnsdall stayed in Europe. Lloyd Wright sent her an aerial photograph in April as proof of activity on the hill [31]. The prospect of her return—as well as Wright's—pushed Schindler to a feverish state. "Need all doors at once," he wired Weldon & Glasson on May 20. "Situation desperate." Wright arrived in Los Angeles late that month. His "finishing hand" was more than a year late, and he planned to sail again for Japan at the end of July. Back at Taliesin by June 14, he began to barrage Schindler and

Clarence Thomas with telegrams. Sometimes he sent several in a single day. Thomas was embarrassed by cost overruns and had tightened his grip. The house was neither finished nor furnished. Thomas thought Wright was using devious means to get the furniture made; he wrote Miss Barnsdall to warn her. He sent a copy of the letter to Wright, who responded with a telegram:

Your letter a malicious misrepresentation intended for Miss Barnsdall's consumption, not mine. Am calling your petty bluff. Schindler will turn over furniture details, schedules and quality samples to you. Get busy with your little monkey-wrench. Again your stupid egotism and envious insolence interferes with my work to the loss of both work and owner. Your statement concerning the terraces is a lie on its face. You will go ahead with nothing. I withdraw my propositions wholly. Now damn you, make good.

As if Schindler needed a lesson in combat, Wright sent him a transcript of the telegram on June 16, adding that Thomas' letter was "written to deliberately disaffect Miss B. in every possible way that would occur to a coyote like him—his eyes were not set close together and crossed—for nothing." The same letter to Schindler, however, betrayed that Wright *was* working in devious ways:

Now, help me nail his implications and interferences there where our client can see them as they are. If he doesn't get down under us now he's lost. Act quickly and completely to the hilt.

Say nothing of the work completed already at Barker Bros. [the furniture] or he will get straw bids—If he does, I will take the Barker Bros. work and call his bluff again . . . *We* will handle my work in toto or *he* will. This may be as good a way as any to show Miss B. what we have done for her if we can force this monkey-wrench for once—to play fair and stay on the burr. He is contemptible in point of character, ability or anything else . . . .

Miss Barnsdall cabled Lloyd Wright from London that she would send $20,000. "Don't exceed this," she said, "unless agree to deduct from [the architect's] percentage. Can't return until house completed. Check up with Thomas. Cut out dining-room furniture if necessary." Only a garbled copy reached Wright in Wisconsin; by the time Schindler repeated the message, on June 23, Thomas had said the money already was spent.

Wright demanded an audit of Thomas' accounts. "What I saw in Los Angeles," he noted in a memorandum, "con-

31. Hollyhock House under construction, 1921, looking northwest; Residence "A" is toward right, Residence "B" toward upper left.

vinced me that the waste of money and time on that work [has been] no less than criminal—chargeable (they will try to show) to the impotence of the architect. But I shall refuse to take blame because advice rejected. Expect to prove excessive cost of all items in the building . . .." The additional $20,000 would have made all the difference, he telegraphed Schindler on June 27. Wright planned to return to Olive Hill to modify the colors in the house with what he called "slight glazes." (The plaster wall and ceiling surfaces, according to the specifications, were to be stained with a "mixture of boiled linseed oil, turpentine and melted beeswax colored with oil ground pigments as directed.")

Time was running out. Miss Barnsdall already had left Europe. On June 27, Wright wrote her a long cry from the heart:

If I would see you face to face before I sail for Japan, July 30th, I would not write. But somehow I don't believe I will see you. I think you would prefer to go quietly into your home alone. I expect to personally put the finishing work upon it from July 14th to July 30th.

You will marvel then, perhaps, as I do, that a thing so harmonious, strong and unlike anything of its kind in the world—should be there at all. That this creative thing should have survived the petty personal strife that "dogged" its growth, step by step, is a miracle. You will feel this yourself, perhaps, as the echoes reach you before you reach its threshold.

Order shall come out of chaos for you—because the principle at stake is dearer to me than my humiliations are bitter: and because your devotion to it was stronger than your own resentment or the power of misrepresentation and the alarmist advice of unwilling, unfaithful amateurs that threatened it during construction and crowding in upon it even now.

I have had to use weapons to do my part and am ashamed, not proud, of my use of them. Even *this* use of them will be used against me as *proof* of the insulting references that I am morally oblique that caused me to use the weapons. I did write a "hell-of-a-letter" to

Clarence Thomas that was oversized for his case. But it only mildly expressed my feeling. He has hindered my work, protecting himself by pretending to guard your interests. Alone, absolutely against the field, I have all but achieved the impossible. I have battled the thing out *almost* to a finish.

But I have not had one man I could trust, from first to last, or that I could depend upon as expert to understand and push along behind me, since Robertson showed himself incompetent.

I needed a veteran builder familiar with this original type of building. I needed him because the whole is an invention, the details to the smallest, all inventions. Imagination and enthusiasm and experience and loyalty should meet in the builder at my back, or the difficulties of my work be turned against me as sins of omission, or evasion or incompetence. You were led by self-serving advice to assume that what amateurs could see and understand of the usual thing in the *usual* way was what should apply to me and my way of work. The superiority and distinction you sought when you came to me was to "happen" somehow, as a gift to you, no matter how you tied me up? . . .

I made an initial mistake in haste which was unavoidable, in choosing Robertson, under circumstances beyond my control—and—after doing all I could to rectify the mistake you have held it over and against me ever since by your man Thomas . . . .

There was no interest in the life of the building itself on anyone's part but my own. You had taken the stand that my services were one thing and building the building another thing. The one was mine, the other was yours. But I must be responsible for both. Why this absurdity? . . .

You probably assumed that I would protect my work at any trouble or cost to me or at any cost to you. The building has come near to what you hoped and dreamed it would be only because, in this assumption, you were correct.

I did protect it as well as I could.

But has this been any fairer to me than to yourself? . . . My soul is sore and my mind stiff with insults. I have devoted more personal time, energy and money to this work, three times over than was necessary: Crossed the Pacific twice to keep faith with you—at great sacrifice to other interests entrusted to me . . .

It does seem as though the execution of the design was business and the conception of it art. But in my experience both are allied and both in a sense art . . .

Additional costs will all be attributed to my "changes" instead of to the bad-method and wasteful ignorance of the nature of the work on the part of the men you forced me to work with . . . Los Angeles was a strange new field for me and I had to literally "break into" it. Apparently they did not want me out there and do not want me now.

Discord between owner and architect soon became known to the workmen and the fact also that the owner—"rich"—was "holding the bag"—building her own building—herself. Why then should they worry—and they didn't worry. You did. And I did.

Nobody really cared to protect the rich woman or understand the freak architect and his fool-work anyway; It was to laugh at him—"Queer get up, his. No doubt a faker." Stories about his private life on the Q.T. And hers.—"Say, the man must simply be a wonder to get away with it?" "Well, let him get it over on the woman if he can. We'll see the fun!"

I lost my temper. Often. I have a caustic way of meeting my adversaries . . .

The work I do is not drawing-board Architecture. I must have my own privileges in the field where any battle is inevitably fought and eventually won or lost . . . For this margin in the field I should have a competent fund, which experience has taught me should be between fifteen and twenty percent on work like yours . . .

Just think for a moment of another phase. There was "Kirah," Roy George, Clarence Thomas, Robertson, Hickey et al., others you alluded to. Ordynski perhaps. Kind, fatuous old Mr. Ray. Your "faithful attorney." Norm Geddes et al. Miss Lang, Susan, too, and how many others all openly or subtly or tentatively or suggestively hostile to any real understanding between you and me. All professing particolored fears for unprotected Aline in the "Den of the wolf." I did not know what a really terrible fellow I was until it began to crop up and surround you in this heroic and genuinely purposeful effort of your life . . . you struck at the only one who could have saved you and that was *"the Wolf"* himself. Your whole fair project of the Hill poisoned at its source for you. I could not save you. By a miracle only will I be able to save the building . . .

Well—the building stands. Your home.

It is yours for what it has cost you. It is mine for what it has cost me.

And it is for all mankind according to its cost in all its bearings.

Can we not pronounce benediction upon it, now, absolving the building itself at least from rancour and false witness?

Whatever its birth pangs it will take its place as your contribution and mine to the vexed life of our time. What future it will have—maimed as it is—who can say?

Schindler learned that Miss Barnsdall was headed back from England and due in Los Angeles by July 10. "Impossible to complete building," he telegraphed Wright on July 1. Wright immediately left Taliesin for New York, apparently to intercept her. Residence "A" was finished that first week of July at a cost of more than $20,000, or nearly the amount Miss Barnsdall once expected to spend for her own residence. Hollyhock House cost about $125,000, a Hollywood newspaper reported.[14] The cabinetwork and trim alone, Lloyd Wright recalled in 1945, had cost more than $25,000. On July 6 the planing mill burned down; Weldon & Glasson resumed work July 22 at a new plant and the millwork continued into August. Schindler told the plastering con-

tractor on August 5 that the upstairs bedrooms were not to be finished: Miss Barnsdall refused to spend any more money. The outer walls of the house were stained in September to a light gray-green—"lighter than the cast stone," Lloyd Wright said, "for contrast." The color was meant to suggest the subtle tint of olive leaves. It would also perfectly complement the pink and red flowers Miss Barnsdall intended to plant. By then, however, she already was traveling again in Europe.

Wright was back in Japan. Schindler said that he too was anxious for the end. "I shall take a vacation presently in order to restore my equilibrium," he wrote Wright on September 13, "and hope after that to [be] able to think about something else besides patches, leaks and contracts." In October he left for Yosemite. The rooms on the second story were bare, and the chamber lacked its porch or any opening to the north. The art-stone walls of the balcony off the owner's room awkwardly conflicted with the stucco walls of the rest of the house. Much of the leaded glass for doors and windows never was made, nor was some of the furniture. The library had no skylight, and the roof terraces had no finished flooring in tile.

Hollyhock House was abandoned, not finished. And yet, as Wright said, a strangely beautiful form had appeared. "There was nothing like it anywhere in the world," he wrote.[15]

---

[14] *Hollywood Citizen News*, July 8, 1921.

[15] Wright, *An Autobiography*, p. 233.

"NOTHING LIKE IT ANYWHERE"

HOLLYHOCK HOUSE TOO OFTEN is called "Mayan": Whether by instinct or poor education, the mind tries to accommodate the original by taking refuge in the familiar. Nothing so clouds sight, however, as a style concept. Memory is no substitute for imagination, and history is not art.

The major buildings of the Maya often stood on mounds, made use of stucco along with stone, magnified their scale by small and widely spaced wall openings, sometimes formed courtyards and generally flourished in strong contrasts of sun and shade. All are possible points of comparison. The tall upper walls of Hollyhock House—pitched at 85 degrees, or a slope defined by the drawings as one inch to the foot—can bring to mind the flying facades, or false fronts, of Mayan architecture. But in fact they are parapets for the roof terraces. The ornaments in the frieze also might be mistaken as clues to history; but their lighthearted spirit is opposite that of the crabbed and airless carvings of the Maya. The second story could suggest the Mayan roof-comb, so aptly described as "a veritable headdress of masonry."[1] Or the main doorway, shaped as a corbeled or false arch, in which a keystone is superfluous, might seem Mayan; yet the same shape appears in the ancient architecture of the Mediterranean.

As a young architect, Wright presumably encountered the replicated "Ruins of Yucatan" at the World's Columbian Exposition of 1893, in Chicago, where he could have seen and absorbed just as easily the style of "Old Vienna," a "Javanese Settlement" or a "Bedouin Encampment."[2] The charm of the Maya, then as now, was that of the exotic. Even the homey *Craftsman* magazine in 1906 ran an account that conjured the "immense mysteries of masonry so profoundly screened by mahogany and cedar jungles."[3] Yet the great traveler John Lloyd Stephens had identified as early as 1841 precisely what Wright would come to admire in Mayan architecture. Of the vast ruins, Stephens said there was nothing in Europe like them, because they spoke of a civilization "not derived from the Old World, but originating and growing up here, without models or masters, having a distinct, separate, independent existence; like the plants and fruits of the soil, indigenous."[4]

Thus the formidable irony that Wright faced: Because American architecture was so pervaded by echoes of Europe, whatever he conceived in Hollyhock House was bound to be mistaken as exotic, not indigenous. In 1917, an entire issue of the *Architectural Record* was given to American country houses, described as "picturesque shingled houses, Colonial houses of various types, Renaissance villas, a Hispano-Pueblo house, two Jacobean houses, one house with Francis

---

[1] Pál Kelemen, *Art of the Americas* (New York, 1969), p. 20.

[2] Also known as the "Ruins of Uxmal," they were made of staff (a blend of plaster of Paris with hemp fibers and Portland cement) from papier-mâché molds, and were exhibited near the Dairy Building.

[3] William Griffith, "Tikal—The First American Civilization: 'Skyscrapers' Over One Thousand Years Old Discovered in Yucatan," *Craftsman*, Sept. 1906, p. 689.

[4] J. L. Stephens, *Incidents of Travel in Central America, Chiapas & Yucatan* (Dover reprint, New York, 1969), vol. 2, p. 438.

I. detail, and a few to which it is hard to give a style name."[5] A group of picturesque houses built at the time of Hollyhock House, and not far from it, bore similar witness. One of the architects was Walter Davis, wrote a correspondent for *House Beautiful*:

> I asked Mr. Davis just what the architecture really was. "French peasant?" I ventured. "Near enough," he answered, man-like. "It's now and here. It's modern. We speak of Italian Renaissance—maybe it came from Rome, but it's modern, and there you are!"[6]

Men more or less adept at trading in styles dominated American architecture. What was anyone to make of Hollyhock House? In July 1921, just before Miss Barnsdall arrived in Los Angeles to see her new house, a newspaper described it as "Egyptian"; another newspaper agreed, but said it was also "reminiscent of a dignified estate of an ancient Greek ruler." A few years later, one writer said the house reminded him of a certain Renaissance villa in Venice, but another identified the style as "semi-Oriental." Even the architect H. P. Berlage, who had understood Wright's prairie work better than anyone else, wrote that Hollyhock House was a country house in which "Eastern influences" were at work.[7]

"Working in styles is not architecture," Montgomery Schuyler said in an early appreciation of Wright's contribution.[8] The imagination assimilates, Wright declared, but does not imitate. Where would one look for the indigenous if not in the primitive? Wright had long admired the rigorous lectures of Viollet-le-Duc; corrupted styles can never regenerate architecture, Viollet asserted, and "only primitive sources can furnish the energy for a long career."[9] Wright saw in the architecture of the Maya a primitive abstraction of earth-forms, free from the classical grammar of European architecture, gigantic in mass and often grand in extension:

> Had I not loved and comprehended preColumbian architecture as the primitive basis of world-architecture, I could not now build with the understanding of all architecture. Only with that understanding could I have shaped my buildings as they are. Yet, of all ancient buildings, wherever they may stand or whatever their time, is there one of them suitable to stand here and now in the midst of our time, our America, our machine-age technique? Not one.[10]

The age of the machine and high-strength steel, Wright said, put an end to the claims of classical architecture, but primitive post-and-beam structure would always remain valid. Hollyhock House, he said, takes a holiday from the machine. The wall openings for windows and doors express the most simple order of construction with great beauty, and the second-story bridge (which relies on hidden steel beams) reaches across the east front like a colossal lintel.

Hollyhock House is no more Mayan than such landmarks from earlier in Wright's career as the Avery Coonley house in Riverside, Illinois, or the Midway Gardens in Chicago. It is in fact closer to the Indian architecture of the Southwest. In 1915, Schindler toured the Southwest and found what he called the "first buildings in America which have a real feeling for the ground which carries them."[11] He soon designed an adobe country-house project with sloped walls, slight openings for windows and a square pool in front of the living room. One wing was to comprise the dining room, kitchen and servants' rooms; another, the guest rooms and owner's bedroom. All were to shape a central court flanked by covered walkways. After he arrived in Los Angeles late in 1920, Schindler wrote to his friend Richard Neutra:

> When I speak of American architecture I must say at once that really there is none. There are a few beginnings but architecture has never been wedded to America . . . The only buildings which testify to the deep feeling for [the] soil on which they stand are the sunbaked adobe buildings of the first immigrants and their successors—Spanish and Mexican—in the southwestern part of the country.[12]

One early description of Hollyhock House, published in September 1921, thus can claim to be singularly wellinformed, whether by Schindler or Lloyd Wright:

> Think of a good size pueblo on one of New Mexico's mesas or low clean bluffs seen in some parts of the foothills of the Sierras. Refine the outline somewhat, without losing [its] strength, tint it as near an approach as possible to the silver green slopes of these same foothills and bower it with verdure, and you will approach the conception of Miss Barnsdall's home.[13]

5 A. D. F. Hamlin, in the *Architectural Record*, Oct. 1917, p. 309.
6 Edna Goit Brintnall, "Transplanting Atmosphere: A Group of French Peasant Houses Near Hollywood, California," *House Beautiful*, Oct. 1921, p. 281.
7 H. P. Berlage, in *The Life-Work of the American Architect Frank Lloyd Wright* (Santpoort, Holland, 1925–26; new edition, New York, 1965), p. 84. The other descriptions appear in the *Hollywood Citizen News*, July 8, 1921; *Holly Leaves*, July 9, 1921; Fred Hogue, in the *Los Angeles Times*, July 2, 1928; and Emmy Matt Rush, "The Story of an Art Center that Grew Upon a Hilltop," *Overland Monthly and Out West*, new series, May 1930, p. 158.
8 M. Schuyler, "An Architectural Pioneer," *Architectural Record*, Apr. 1912, p. 429.
9 E. E. Viollet-le-Duc, *Discourses on Architecture*, trans. Henry Van Brunt (Boston, 1875), p. 227.

10 Wright, letter of 1953 to the *Magazine of Art*, pub. in Dmitri Tselos, "Frank Lloyd Wright and World Architecture," *Journal of the Society of Architectural Historians*, March 1969, p. 72.
11 Esther McCoy, *Five California Architects* (New York, 1960), p. 153.
12 Esther McCoy, *Vienna to Los Angeles: Two Journeys* (Santa Monica, Calif., 1979), p. 129. For the adobe country-house project, see David Gebhard, *Schindler* (New York, 1971), pp. 28–29.
13 *Hollywood Citizen News*, Sept. 2, 1921.

32. Olive Hill, looking predominantly north; Vermont Avenue at right, Edgemont Street at left.

33. West front. (Ezra Stoller © Esto)

34. West front of living room. (Ezra Stoller © Esto)

In his wash perspective drawings, Lloyd Wright presented the house as a long, low profile upon a mesa; more than 50 years later, he said Hollyhock House was meant to offer a mesa silhouette like those originated by the pueblo dwellers.[14] Wright himself wrote of the house as "a silhouette up there on Olive Hill"; and on a photograph of the ornament at the south living-room door he penciled the title "Desert Abstraction."[15] Olive Hill appears from nowhere, like a mesa high above the desert floor; it rises more than 110 feet above the intersection of Sunset Boulevard with Edge-

mont Street. Miss Barnsdall knew the house would exceed her needs and indeed her desires. No ordinary house could hold the hill or even begin to grace it. Hollyhock House finds its place near the center of the hill and, by honoring the cardinal points, conforms both to Indian cosmography and the street grid [32]. The west front assumes the formality of a pavilion with symmetrical wings [33]. In the center, of course, is the living room, the only room of the house in grand scale [34]. The house embraces Olive Hill with such care that it leaves free the highest point of the site, slightly to

[14] *Los Angeles Herald-Examiner*, Oct. 17, 1975, p. A-3. Eric Lloyd Wright has commented that his father "always talked about Southwest—not Maya—Indians." John Lloyd Wright also admired Indian structures of the Southwest; see *My Father Who Is on Earth* (New York, 1946; Dover reprint, 1992), p. 131.

[15] The photograph is catalogued as 1705.026 in the Frank Lloyd Wright Archives. Wright refers to the house as a silhouette in *An Autobiography*

(New York, 1943), p. 224; on p. 309 he declares that the "great nature-masonry we see rising from the great mesa floors is all the noble architecture Arizona has to show at present and that is not architecture at all. But it is inspiration." In *The Life-Work of the American Architect*, p. 59, he writes, "I feel in the silhouette of the Olive Hill house a sense of the romance of the region . . . ."

35. Early view of south front, looking northeast.

the east and just above the exedra.[16] In this gentlest of ways, Hollyhock House crowns the hill. The ornaments of the frieze become the jewels of the crown.

The south front stretches across the hill like a living creature, as the Indians believe their pueblos to be, and fairly bristles with rooms and walled terraces projecting into the landscape [35, 36]. Seven rooms in fact share in this front, and the stepped massing evokes the spirit of an abiding earth-architecture [37]. In the openings of the living room and

[16] Contrary to a commonplace criticism, the house does not violate Wright's rule that "no house should ever be *on* a hill or *on* anything. It should be *of* the hill." See *An Autobiography* (New York, 1943), p. 168. The lawn at the top of the exedra is at an elevation of 488.5 feet above sea level. The datum of the house is set at 483.5 feet, and the garden court is at 487 feet. The datum of the theater was to be 405 feet.

library, post-and-lintel structure attains monumental simplicity [38]. To the east, the conservatory hunches to the ground to become continuous with the south patio wall [39]. Its floor is four steps below that of the guest rooms, which rise still higher to form parapets for a roof terrace [40]. Across the patio, the child's room also expresses post-and-lintel with great elegance and strength, but in a different way [41]. The southeast corner of the house is the most assertively developed of all its exterior aspects [42]. The child's room expands into a playroom, the owner's room opens to a balcony above it, and both bedroom suites glory in an east bay resplendent in leaded-glass windows [43]. The bay furnishes the owner with a sleeping porch and the child with a dressing room. It recalls the finest work of Wright's earlier years because the expression is so characteristic: The roof is can-

36. South faces of living room and library; conservatory obscured by wall. (Ezra Stoller © Esto)

37. Early view of library and conservatory, looking predominantly east.

RIGHT, TOP: 38. Living room, library and conservatory, looking north. RIGHT, MIDDLE: 39. Conservatory and west guest room, looking northwest. OPPOSITE: 40. Early view of guest rooms, looking northwest. RIGHT, BOTTOM: 41. Child's room, looking east.

42. Owner's quarters and playroom, looking northeast.

44. East front, looking southwest; highest point of hill is the lawn at lower left. (Ezra Stoller © Esto)

43. Early view of east bay, looking southwest; nursemaid's room and exedra at right.

tilevered; massive, pierlike forms below it stop short of affording any structural support, and, in consequence of this calculated tension, the upper corners fly open.

Miss Barnsdall recognized the importance of the bay; it established that face of the house as an east front, not the back [44, 45]. The east front not only comprises three bedrooms, the nursemaid's room, two other servants' rooms and the owner's wardrobe and trunk room. It presides over the long passage from the living room across the loggia, through the garden court, under the bridge and past the fountain pool and exedra to the flowered path toward what was to be the promenade above the theater. Wright's first sketches already show a tall pine grove parted at the center to honor this major axis, or ceremonial causeway, from the owner's residence to her new theater.[17] From the east, the pine grove and enclosing eucalyptus walk repeat at a higher elevation the massing of the theater. From other perspectives, the trees form a backdrop to the house. They also culminate the steps in elevation from the west lawn to the living-room roof and the

[17] In noting the terraces of the house as well as this sense of a causeway, Elpidio Rocha, a Los Angeles educator and planner, finds parallels with the plan of Tenochtitlán, ancient capital of the Aztecs.

roof of the bridge. Once again the top of the hill is given to nature, the trees.

From the north, much of the house is screened by gardens, flowering shrubs and the kitchen-yard wall, six and one-half feet tall [46]. The north front accommodates arrival and entrance. It also affords splendid vistas toward the Hollywood Hills, not far off, and toward Griffith Park [47]. Two extensions flank the motor court and greatly distinguish the north front. One is the chain of animal pens, a pet pergola that leads all the way to the chauffeur's quarters and garage, a distance of about 190 feet [48]. The other, in a reach of more than 90 feet, comprises the entrance loggia, porte-cochere, niche and a garden wall terminated with a flower urn [49]. In plan, these extraordinary extensions can easily be seen as abstractions of the tall plant for which the house is named. They also express the house as an organism vitally attached to the hill. Hollyhock House, like a sculpture in the round, has many aspects and no single front. The west face is the most formal, but the north face affords the entrance; the east face embraces the highest point of the site and offers a view into the garden court, while the south face is the most active of all.

RIGHT: 45. South servant's room (center) and north chamber (upper right), looking west. BELOW: 46. Motor court, looking southwest toward porte-cochere and entrance loggia. (Ezra Stoller © Esto)

BELOW: 47. Early view of motor court and garage, looking predominantly north. LEFT: 48. Early view of animal pens, looking predominantly north.

49. Early view of house, looking southeast.

PASSAGES, ROOMS
AND COURTS

HOLLYHOCK HOUSE FORMS a quadrangle to sequester an inner garden court, but reaches outward to consort with as much of the world as it can [50]. Wright can invest one and the same building with a profound sense of shelter and an exhilarating air of excursion into the American landscape. That is his great achievement. Hollyhock House is not so much ambivalent as comprehensive; it can respond to every rhythm of the day, every slight change in the spirit.

The plan creates a confederation of rooms which belong to a definite whole but secede from one another as if engaged in widespread declarations of independence [51, 52]. Hollyhock House refuses to support the tiresome gloss about Wright, that the rooms of his houses blend marvelously together and space is miraculously made to flow. Not only are its rooms distinct and equipped with heavy doorway curtains, or portieres, for further privacy; often the rooms do not even touch one another. Long passageways separate the very rooms they ostensibly serve to connect. Intermediate alcoves allow the music room and library to keep their distance from the living room, which stands virtually as a pavilion unto itself. The library turns a blind wall to deflect attention into the living room, and the dining room retreats to an unexpected place, obliquely across the entry hall and up four steps. The conservatory, peculiarly removed from the kitchen if used as a breakfast room, occupies a small world of its own.

R. M. Schindler knew what to expect; he had lived at Taliesin and at Wright's earlier home and studio in Oak Park. "His buildings are organisms in which every part or member finds its natural expression," he wrote Richard Neutra soon after arriving in Los Angeles, "and they are compositions in which each form resounds through the whole building or finds its harmonies."[1]

The plan of Hollyhock House also shows a fine disregard for the tyranny of an axis. It takes delight, conversely, in occult balance rather than static symmetry. Wright puts to play Louis Sullivan's perception of the difference between symmetrical forms and "others purely rhythmical."[2] The major axis of the living room soon encounters an asymmetrical garden court; the axis of the entry hall collides with the east corners of the living room, and the axis of the music room and library gets blocked by the south alcove wall. Through such calculated liberties, Wright generates the rhythms and perspectives that charm the eye. Similarly, an early study of the plan on a four-foot grid may have served as a guide to proportions, but it did not represent a mechanical system of design or an accurate table of dimensions. The working drawings strayed from the grid and remained subject to revision; during construction, room measurements strayed from the working drawings. In such ways, the house makes bold to disdain the precision that strikes the eye as

---

[1] McCoy, *Vienna to Los Angeles*, p. 130.
[2] Louis H. Sullivan, *Kindergarten Chats and Other Writings* (Dover reprint, New York, 1979), p. 45.

50. Hollyhock House in 1924, looking northeast; child on living-room roof may be Sugartop.

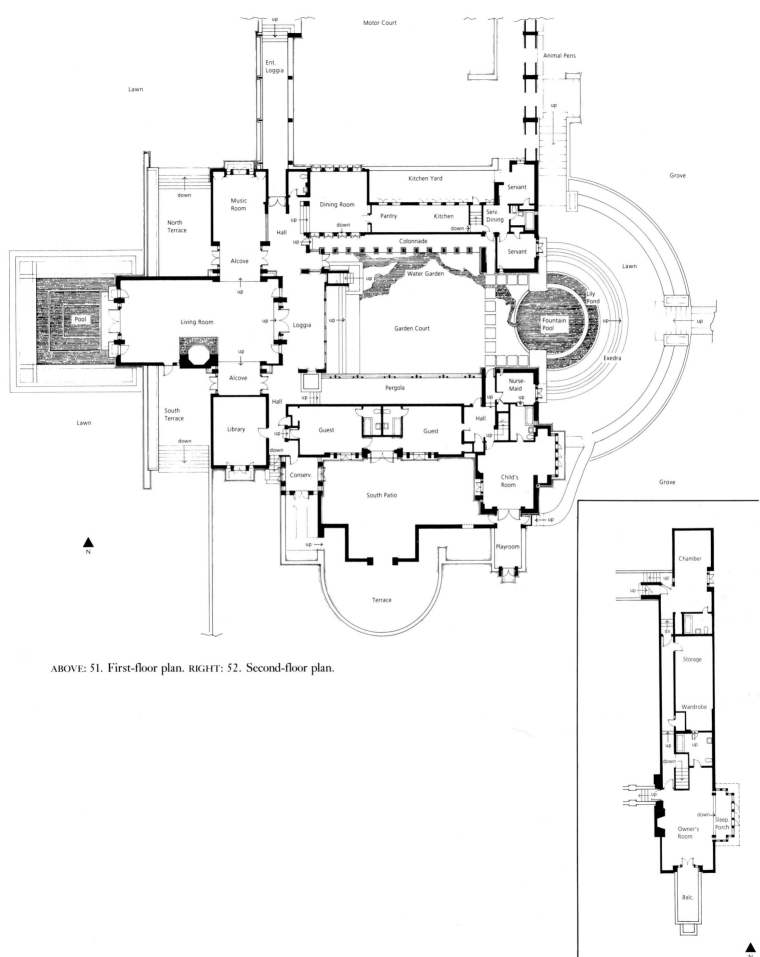

ABOVE: 51. First-floor plan. RIGHT: 52. Second-floor plan.

cold. It welcomes the pleasurable irregularities by which we quickly identify an individual.[3] On close approach, moreover, the scale of the house relaxes. It changes almost magically from grandeur to intimacy.

The long entrance loggia, a roofed but open gallery, trips along the west side of the motor court to greet those who arrive at the porte-cochere, a streamlined carriage-porch [53]. The flat canopy of the porte-cochere, cantilevered more than 28 feet to the north and nearly ten feet to the east, casts into soft shade the marble Chinese garden sculpture of a bodhisattva, once so happily at home within the niche but later moved indoors [54].

Much about the house can be forecast from the niche, porte-cochere and entrance loggia. Two characteristic details give the niche its exceptional energy and articulation: the frequent corners or returns at the base and the graphic wood strips at the ceiling. Corners are the traps in a foursquare, confining room. By multiplying them, paradoxically, into a

[3] The plan sketch on a grid is catalogued as 1705.33 in the Frank Lloyd Wright Archives. The music room can serve as an example of the deviations. In the unit system it measures 16 by 16 feet; in the working drawings of Sept. 1921, it is 18 feet by 16 feet; and as constructed it measures 19½ feet by 15 feet, 9 inches.

darting pattern of swift turns, Wright sets a space free.⁴ The wood strips—what Lloyd Wright nicely called stripe-moldings—also animate the space; by leading the eye quickly from one plane to the next they establish a free community of surfaces.

The porte-cochere holds even more significance: It is either a sunshade or an anomaly. Under the warm southern California sky, Wright has no reason to repeat the roofs he so forcefully cantilevered in his prairie architecture. Yet the cantilevered roof, which both expressed and provided shelter, had been his most vigorous agent in making a building belong to the landscape. What can take its place? His answer is to create various and odd rifts in the walls, unexpected and delightful openings to the outdoors. The first appears in the west wall of the niche [55]. A strange shape, it can be seen either as a step pyramid or as an inverted corbel arch: allusions to an archaic earth-architecture. Another opening of odd profile occurs five times in the west wall of the entrance loggia, and gives the wall its redoubled rhythm [56]. The east wall of the loggia opens broadly through a trellis of wood

OPPOSITE, BOTTOM: 53. Porte-cochere and entrance loggia, looking southwest. (Ezra Stoller © Esto) OPPOSITE, TOP: 54. Early view of niche at porte-cochere, with bodhisattva, looking west. ABOVE, LEFT: 55. Niche without bodhisattva, looking west. ABOVE: 56. View from entrance loggia, looking predominantly west.

⁴ After her first visit to Taliesin, in 1924, Dione Neutra wrote that it had "innumerable corners." See *Richard Neutra: Promise and Fulfillment, 1919–1932*, p. 127.

57. Entrance loggia, looking south.

rails, pitched to reflect the upper walls of the house as well as the shape of the playroom, the major extension of the house diagonally opposite. By casting patterns of sun and shadow, both walls enliven the loggia floor. Through its strong rhythms, its elevation of six steps above the motor court— one step now submerged by a later paving—and the stature of its proportions (taller than wide, and extended nearly 37 feet from the top step to the art-stone entryway), the loggia becomes a ceremonial approach [57]. The narrowed passage to the front doors, like the niche, is lighted at night from a patterned ceiling screen of wood [58]. Punctuated by slits of glass through which visitors can be observed, the art-stone doors are sparingly ornamented with lock covers of cast brass, designed by Schindler four years after the house was built. The doors turn on pintles, slowly but with surprising ease.

The entry hall and loggia (in some drawings called the porch) are only passages, too; yet passages that offer a complex range of choices. The ceiling height is six feet, eight inches: higher than usual for Wright, but low in relation to the length of the spaces, for the vista from the front doors to the guest room wall reaches 56 feet [59]. Within that distance are eight possibilities of lateral movement. To the east is the dining room, up four steps [60]. Another destination can be the lavatory, hidden by the entryway (and later removed for a staircase). The music room, opposite the dining-room steps, is partly screened by a wood grille of rhythmically spaced stiles, and cannot be entered until one reaches the glass doors

58. Entrance, looking south.

59. Early view of loggia, looking south; relief carving from Tripoli at left.

of the north alcove [61]. A glass door near the steps to the dining room opens to the colonnade at the north side of the garden court. Originally, paired casements looked over the water garden [62]. The loggia leads to steps up to the pergola and also to the doors of the south alcove; primarily, however, it serves as a vestibule between the living room and garden court. It originally opened to the court through folding glass doors, a subtle complement to the Japanese folding screens installed in the living room, music room and south alcove [63]. The west wall of the loggia repeats the west wall of the living room as an extended screen, an intricate and lively sequence of leaded-glass casements and fixed panels (some only four inches wide) spaced by hollyhock columns and art-stone posts ornamented only on the sides [64, 65].

The living room, one step down from the alcoves and loggia, is the only room of the house in grand scale: more than three times the size of any other room. It nevertheless seems the most secluded and protective [66]. The few openings in its walls and ceiling, the bas-relief sculpture above the

LEFT: 60. Early view into dining room, looking northeast; chandelier obviously not of Wright's design. ABOVE: 61. Entry, looking west into music room, with clerestory above steps to dining room.

62. Early view from entry hall toward water garden, looking east.

OPPOSITE, TOP: 63. Early view through folding doors of loggia, looking east. OPPOSITE, BOTTOM LEFT: 64. Detail of wall screen between loggia and living room, looking predominantly west. OPPOSITE, BOTTOM RIGHT: 65. Art-stone column in loggia, looking northwest. ABOVE: 66. Living room with furniture ensemble as reconstructed in 1990, looking west.

fireplace and the inglenook formed by the grand ensemble of furniture all function to orient the room to the south and west [67]. The room indeed means to speak of the Southwest; its colors are mainly the quiet pastels of desert earth tones and brave desert plants.

A study for the furniture layout shows the living room to be a double square [68].[5] The fireplace plan, which echoes in

[5] Wright thought the square signified integrity. Olive Hill is square in plan, and the house as a whole, in forming a quadrangle, responds to its site. A drawing of August 1946 by Lloyd Wright, for the 1947 rebuilding of the house, gives the living-room dimensions as 23 feet by 46 feet, confirming the intention of a square. Typically, a working drawing of August 1920 gives dimensions of 24 feet by 46½ feet, and the room in fact measures 23 feet, eight inches by 46 feet, one inch.

miniature the proposed theater, is an octagon: a square with the corners cut off. The inglenook seats, angled at 45 degrees, imply squares sliced in half. The doors in the west wall form a square opening to the balcony, which overlooks a pool of squares inscribed within squares; the opposite opening, in the wall screen between the living room and loggia, is also square. Finally, a double square becomes the format for the sculptured fireplace front [69, 70].

The bas-relief at the fireplace is composed in blocks of art-stone and ranks among the few and great mural abstractions that Wright designed. Strictly geometric, monochromatic and austere in pattern, it is at the same time rich in references. The circles resound with the shape of the south

67. Early view of living room, looking southwest.

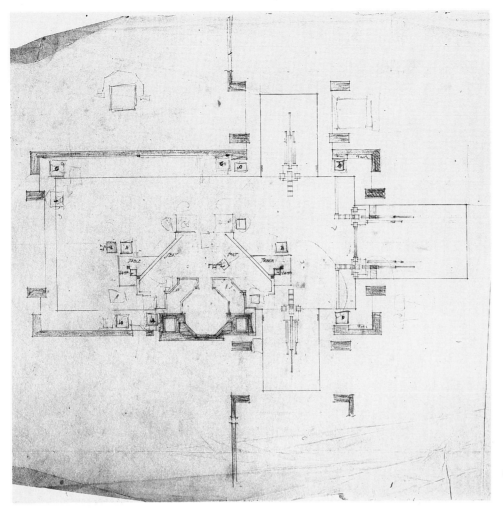

68. Study for living-room furniture layout.

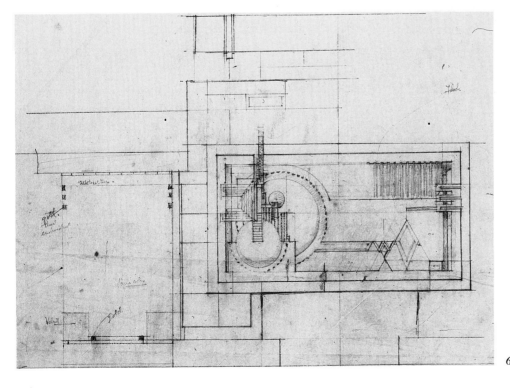

69. Drawing for fireplace front.

RIGHT: 70. Fireplace front, looking south. BELOW: 71. Early view of living room, looking northwest.

terrace and the fountain pool at the far end of the garden court. The tall shaft breaks through the double square as another hollyhock abstraction. Behind it, compound rectangles are broken to create the profiles of step pyramids and false arches. Across the top of the mural, a row of stiles recalls the wood screen at the entry. The cluster of equilateral triangles plays on the design of the dining-room table, in which a hexagonal top rests upon a triangular pedestal. Beyond all these geometrical allusions, the mural offers a representational image: a figure seated as if on a throne, looking westward. Wright once ornamented the north wall of his bedroom with the figure of an Indian chief looking out over the Plains. Now he associated his client, too, with the indigenous. "She was as near American as any Indian," Wright wrote in his autobiography. "Up there on Olive Hill above

hillsides furrowed with rows of grey-green olive trees, the daughter of one of America's pioneers had constructed a little principality, her very own, free to live as queen."[6]

A small pool once surrounded the hearth and was bridged by an art-stone step [71]. Fed from the water garden, it carried indoors the sense of an oasis. In turn, it flowed under the living-room floor and into the pool at the west lawn. Gold tiles in the pool by the hearth responded to the gold of the Japanese screens at the west corners of the room, and to the plaster walls of "unevenly tarnished gold" [72].[7] The north

---

[6] Wright, *An Autobiography*, pp. 229, 233. Also see John Lloyd Wright, *My Father Who Is on Earth*, p. 34.

[7] As described by Francis William Vreeland, "A New Art Centre For the Pacific Coast," *Arts & Decoration*, Nov. 1927, p. 64. The *Hollywood Citizen News* reported on Sept. 2, 1921, that Wright already had supplied the house with two Japanese screens of green and gold.

72. Early view of furniture ensemble, looking northwest.

wall originally was blind; by offering no access to the north terrace, it reinforced the privacy and protectiveness of the inglenook [73]. The majestic ensemble of oak furniture—angled seats with cushions in brown frieze, footstools, ottomans, side chairs and tables—rises into torcheres, lamps like flaming torches, more than seven feet tall. They throw light on the ceiling and mediate between its height, nearly 13 feet, and that of the furniture below. An early study reveals how Wright typically develops an idea toward greater strength, not delicate refinement [74]. In the final design, the top of each torchere flares outward as an inverted and truncated pyramid, thus mirroring the ceiling [75].

Oak moldings divide the ceiling into panels tinted a light Nile green, bronze, ochre and terra-cotta. Most of the floor was covered by a rug that extended 58 feet on the longer axis and 40 feet at the crossing of the alcoves [76]. The field color was a light golden brown, and the pattern colors—a light teal blue, dull gold and violet—appeared in yet another hollyhock abstraction, a motif that in each instance climbed a step between the living room and an adjacent space. Schindler wrote W. & J. Sloane of New York to keep in mind first that "the pattern colors shall not form holes in the background but shall come forward, forming spots of brilliance," and second that "the three pattern colors shall be very close together in their carrying power."

Mitered moldings with beadwork of connected and thus incompleted hexagons enframe the wall surfaces and at the

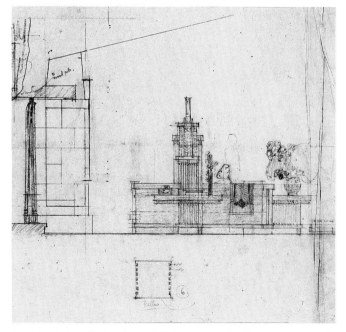

OPPOSITE: 73. Early view of living room, looking east. ABOVE: 74. Study of living-room furniture ensemble and pillow.

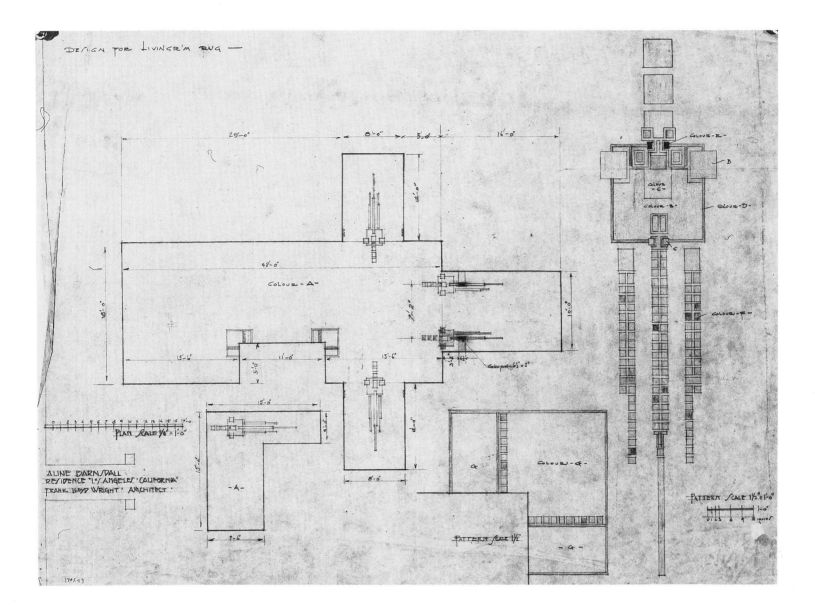

OPPOSITE: 75. Early view of living room, looking southeast. ABOVE: 76. Plan and details for living-room rug.

77. Early view of living room, looking predominantly east.

ABOVE, LEFT: 78. Early view of overstuffed armchair at northeast corner of living room. ABOVE, RIGHT: 79. Window in north alcove, looking west.

same time turn the corners [77]. Unusually broad, the moldings rise two feet above the floor and are 13 inches wide at the openings. Miss Barnsdall had wanted the room paneled in walnut; in the drawings, the walls are indeed shown with horizontal paneling. Instead, the mitered moldings are of white oak and consistent with the furniture. The portieres again were of a brown frieze, back-to-back finished according to the specifications "with appliqué of old violet velvet and gold thread." The window curtains were of Burma cloth. Because the skylight flooded the room with light—at the roof

it was protected only by a second skylight, of wire glass—it too was furnished with portieres. The sturdy oak sidechairs and overstuffed armchairs reflected the characteristic slope of the upper walls [78].

A fixed sash in the north alcove illustrates how Wright enhances nature by presenting it with unexpected loveliness through a geometric pattern of leaded glass [79]. The typical glass design, accented with panes of violet (the color of desert shadows and distant hills), is generated from the 30–60 triangle, a basic drafting tool. Paired, such triangles form an

80. North alcove and music room, looking north.

81. Early view of south alcove, looking south.

equilateral triangle, or one-sixth of a hexagon: the motif for the beadwork and the dining-room table. Hollyhock House takes root, then, in the elementary shapes of the square, the circle and the triangle. The north alcove is a space of passage, only about 11 feet square, and is defined in part by an oak and leaded-glass ceiling light. It connects the living room and the music room, and affords each its only access to the north terrace [80].

By comparison to the living room, the music room not only is subordinate but minor. Miss Barnsdall proposed to decorate the vacant west wall with a Monet—among those she owned was a small painting of water lilies, from 1899— but Wright prevailed, and a Japanese screen was installed instead. When he rebuilt the house in 1947, Lloyd Wright filled the west wall with a row of cabinets about five feet tall, again with hexagonal beadwork and with hexagonal cutouts as door pulls. The opposite wall is largely shaped by a series of low cabinets, which form a shallow bench and support the 33 stiles of the screen at the entry hall. A tall cabinet, identified by an early drawing as the Victrola case, stands as a terminal at the southeast corner of the room. But the eye is inevitably drawn to the north wall of the room, where the tall windows frame a vista past the entrance loggia to Griffith Park.

The vista in the opposite direction ends very soon with the south alcove, a much different space [81]. Unlike the

82. Early view of south alcove, looking southwest.

83. Early view of hall and pergola, looking east.

85. Library windows, looking southwest.

north alcove, it is a place of pause and great serenity. The south wall, 12 feet wide and finished in quiet gold, hides the library and accepts another Japanese screen [82]. Wright here averts the easy symmetry implied by the west front of the house and gives to the wall the ineffable beauty and grace that comes entirely from light. To the east, the doors of the alcove face a massive planter, about six feet square, that marks the steps to the pergola [83]. A bright passage 47 feet long and only seven and one-half feet wide, the pergola originally was roofed in wire glass, with trellis beams meant for vines [84]. The larger beams, eight feet apart, respond to every other pillar in the colonnade by the water garden, and the face of the pergola opens to the garden court through 12

leaded-glass casements of a simple rectilinear pattern. The casements are spaced by large fixed panes of plain glass. Above the art-stone sillcourse of the south wall, leaded-glass transoms and clerestory lights once served the two guest rooms, which had no direct access to the garden court. The pergola thus afforded a private corridor to the owner's rooms.

Viewed from the lawn, the library seems to match the music room; but the plan shows it to be a much more self-contained, even isolated, space. Bookcases consume three of the walls. Left without furniture designed by Wright, and without the small skylight shown in the drawings, the library finds relief only in its windows [85]. They at least protest the confinement of the room by offering a vista past

84. View from pergola into garden court, looking predominantly north.

ABOVE: 86. Conservatory, or breakfast room, with desk by Lloyd Wright; looking south. OPPOSITE: 87. View over conservatory roof and circular terrace, looking southeast.

the long garden wall, which reaches nearly 54 feet into the landscape.

The conservatory, already called the breakfast room in a drawing of August 1920, thrives as a delightful pavilion despite its very modest dimensions, only 12 feet by ten [86]. Lighted from three sides, it opens through French doors to a small and private flower garden. The walk turns east and up three steps to the south circular terrace [87]. The two guest rooms, adjacent to the breakfast room, were nearly identical. Spare in detail, they shared a hipped ceiling as well as French doors to the south patio and terrace [88]. Not many years after the house was built, both rooms were sacrificed to create a gallery for art exhibitions.

Of the eight bedrooms in the house, only the child's room

and owner's room above it are graced with fireplaces. Both rooms also benefit from their inventive turns and openings of the walls. Originally, a built-in seat near the entrance to the child's room was meant to define the cozy domain of the fireplace [89]. At the other side of the room, a wood grille on top of a low partition screens the dressing alcove, a space about 12 feet by six that is lighted by a glorious bay of leaded-glass windows [90]. One of the drawings shows how this mural of nature was to have been complemented by a playful geometric mural above the fireplace, which was never executed. In the same spirit, some of the woodwork in the room is of English holly, a play on the notion of holly wood in Hollywood. Past the window groups and casework, the child's room opens through French doors to a sunny porch

LEFT: 88. Portal to circular terrace, looking predominantly south. BELOW: 89. Child's room, looking southwest.

90. Dressing alcove, looking southeast.

for play [91]. Here the glass walls are pitched at 85 degrees and patterned with triangular designs Lloyd Wright once described as comparable in style to a composition by Gershwin. In all, the child's suite, conveniently connected through the bathroom to the small nursemaid's room at the north, measures more than 37 feet long. The doors at the south end of the playroom open awkwardly to an elevated flower box; but the side doors gave Sugartop secret access to the lawn [92]. Clearly enough, Wright identifies with the child. The doors are only 27 inches wide, and the gate to the south terrace, and its magic of sunlight, is less than five feet high [93].[8]

Garden walls shape the south terrace and patio as outdoor rooms. This congenial conversation between indoor and outdoor spaces particularly impressed an early witness to the life of the house, Barbara Morgan, the photographer:

> Half the beauty of the place is in the relationship of the exterior with the interior. In many rooms glass doors or leaded panels give upon lawns or open corridors, so that at all times the sunlight and greenness, flower and earth fragrance, and birds' singing are somehow present within the house.[9]

Even before the house was built, Miss Barnsdall resisted the owner's suite and planned to sleep in the remote north chamber. She eventually chose to use one of the downstairs guest rooms. The owner's suite has a strange, primitive beauty that probably was much too strong for her tastes [94]. The fireplace looks like a toy construction of oversized artstone blocks, more suited to the child's room; but at the same time it has the elementary power of a sculpture by Brancusi.

---

[8] After meeting Wright for the first time in April 1924, at the funeral of Louis Sullivan, Neutra wrote his wife: "Wright has the head of a lion resting on a rather well proportioned body. He looks about fifty-six, is truly a child, but not a well-behaved one." See *Richard Neutra: Promise and Fulfillment, 1919–1932*, p. 122.

[9] Barbara Morgan, "The California Art Club's New Home," *The Arts*, August 1927, p. 113.

LEFT: 91. View toward playroom, looking southwest. ABOVE: 92. Child's passage to south terraces, looking predominantly east.

LEFT: 93. Child's portal to circular terrace, looking south.
BELOW: 94. Owner's bedroom, looking southwest.

95. Doors to balcony of owner's bedroom, looking south.

Curiously, the grouping of French doors and casements at the south wall is like that in the north wall of Wright's own bedroom in his Oak Park home of many years earlier [95]. The glass patterns, however, were designed in 1925 by Schindler, who used frosted glass for greater privacy. From the balcony, the opening appears even more archaic [96]. The art-stone posts support nothing, and they might be seen as an eerie reference to those in front of a walled corbel arch in the Governor's Palace at Uxmal, a major monument of the Maya. But in fact they create a visual tension entirely charac-teristic of Wright's architecture. The liberation of lintel from posts, which occurs again in the window group of the north chamber, speaks of the same freedom as that asserted by a cantilever. Some early drawings show the balcony doorway with earlike ornamental surrounds; the same motif also was omitted from the openings of the north chamber and from the west door of the owner's room [97]. At the east side of the room, Schindler added a wood grille to screen the sleeping porch, two steps down [98]. This splendid bay faces dawn over what was to have been the site of the theater. The leaded-

OPPOSITE, TOP: 96. Balcony to owner's bedroom, looking north.
ABOVE: 97. Door of owner's bedroom to roof terraces, looking east.
OPPOSITE, BOTTOM: 98. Early view of owner's bedroom as finished
by R. M. Schindler, 1925, looking south.

glass casements, two feet wide and more than seven feet tall, compose a continually changing screen, in dazzling triumph over pictures hung on a wall [99].

To the north, the bathroom opens to a wardrobe and attic trunk room in the bridge. The parallel hall, only three feet wide at the floor, runs along the sloped west wall more than 40 feet from the owner's door to that of the chamber [100]. It climbs two steps, then descends three into the chamber. Miss Barnsdall thought the hall was a "long ugly passage," but it is swiftly functional and well lighted by clerestories. As much cannot be said of the chamber, where the plan approaches a double square only because the room appropriates space meant for a small north porch. Any manner of opening in the

north wall could have relieved the gloom [101]. A narrow door at the west wall opens again to the roof terraces; like the window group in the east wall, it was intended to be of leaded glass. The chamber, almost 250 feet away from morning coffee in the kitchen, does offer a certain privacy.

Of the two servants' rooms below, the south room is the smaller and yet the more appealing. Less than nine by 11 feet, it benefits from a tall leaded-glass casement that opens beneath the bridge, and from a window group addressed eastward toward the center, and highest point, of the hill [102]. A special storage cabinet, sunk beneath the windows, projects well past the plane of the east front. The same feature appears in the nursemaid's room, a nearly identical

OPPOSITE: 99. Sleeping porch, looking east. LEFT: 100. Hall through bridge, looking south into owner's room; note pitched wall at right. BELOW: 101. Chamber, looking northeast; note pitched wall at left.

space at the other side of the bridge; outdoors, the two cabinets become terminals to the exedra, the stepped seating around the fountain pool [see 44]. A leaded-glass casement also graces the small bathroom shared by the servants. In the morning sun, the windowshade can look much like a hanging-scroll painting [103]. The servants also share a small dining room, about eight feet by 12.

The kitchen, across the stairwell and up two steps, originally was lightly defined from the pantry, but in the rebuilding of 1947 the two were joined into a single space 24 feet long and less than eight feet wide [104]. Most of the kitchen detailing dates from that time. Casements open above the paved kitchen yard, seven steps down, where a tall court wall joins the east wall of the dining room in reflecting light into the basement [105]. Miss Barnsdall took special interest in the basement laundry, as she told Wright in November 1920:

And let us take up the equipment for my laundry as soon as I return. One of the comforts that I am looking forward to in my own home is my own laundry, when it will be possible to buy the fine kind of things I desire, knowing they won't be faded & torn to pieces the first time they are washed.

Just east of the kitchen yard, the animal pens stretched north from the servants' quarters to the garage as a chain of 16 links, each unit 12 feet wide and fitted with doors of wire

LEFT: 102. Window group in south servant's room, looking east. BELOW, LEFT: 103. Casement with shade pulled, servants' bathroom; looking predominantly east. OPPOSITE: 104. Kitchen as rebuilt in 1947, looking predominantly west. BELOW, RIGHT: 105. Kitchen yard, looking west.

106. Dining room, looking predominantly north.

mesh in cedar sash. The pet pergola was intended to amuse Sugartop; pens were variously designated for rabbits, fowl and a pony. Other units served as the saddle room, feed room and toolshed. The garage, as an appendage to the house, maintains the same design and anchors the motor court. It comprises a workroom at the west, three bays for cars, a living room and bath for the chauffeur (who was also the cook), a cellar below and a roofed but open porch at the east.

The quadrangle of Hollyhock House, however, ends with the dining room [106]. Everything about the room suggests that Miss Barnsdall planned little if any formal entertaining. Although the dining room is convenient to the kitchen, it is estranged from the living room, and smaller than either the music room or the library. In a house measuring 118 by 136 feet, it is less than 17 feet square. The dining table, moreover, is only four and a half feet across and, as a hexagon, cannot easily be extended. For once, Wright indulges his client's affection for wood paneling: the walls, as well as the

furniture, are entirely of genesero, a Latin American white mahogany known also as primavera. Eleven-inch boards run vertically, in concert with the tall-backed chairs, and are bordered with the typical hexagonal beadwork. Most of the geometric motifs of the house are summarized by the table and chairs. The table base is a hexagon, rotated half a turn from the hexagon of the top; the pedestal, in plan, is an equilateral triangle. The chairs—only slightly more comfortable than they look—have square seats; the front legs are notched to reflect the slope in the upper walls of the house, and the backs have a spine shaped as an abstract hollyhock. Casements set low in the north wall engage the eyes of those who are dining. Clerestories and a deck take the wall to the ceiling. At the south wall, French doors of an equal number open to the colonnade, two steps down [107]. The main way to the garden court, however, is through the folding glass doors of the loggia [108].

Full of invention, beautifully scaled to the human figure,

107. Garden court, looking northwest; dining-room doors behind colonnade.

OPPOSITE, BOTTOM: 108. Early view from loggia into garden court, looking east. ABOVE: 109. Dawn past the bridge. ABOVE, RIGHT: 110. Early view across pool into court, looking predominantly west.

the garden court truly forms the heart of Hollyhock House. Wright had always honored the outdoors as the source of life and health; here, he exalts a common theme of southern California architecture: the gift of water in changing a semi-arid place into a private paradise. In March 1921, when the house was being built, Schindler wanted his friend Neutra to understand:

Wright not only has a sense of gardens but his houses are always a piece of developed and refined environmental space—not imaginable without plants, sky and earth. This should explain to you his windows. They are not wall holes but a dissolution of the building material into a grid—leaded glass—as the ground dissolves and becomes lost in the tree branches.[10]

Between the loggia doors and the crosswalk at the opposite side of the lawn, the court space again approximates a square—into which the pergola, colonnade and staircase lightly intrude. To the east, the upper-story bridge becomes a frame for an idyllic vista [109]. The scene is so picturesque and complete that this opening from the court, paradoxically, reinforces its privacy and its aura of a secret garden [110]. Past the bridge, the steps of the exedra rise to a hemicycle of grass at the center of Olive Hill. Miss Barnsdall's

---

[10] McCoy, *Vienna to Los Angeles*, p. 131.

111. Pergola, looking southwest.

aspirations are quietly expressed by the suggestion of an ancient amphitheater at the highest point of the site.

The pergola stretches across the south side of the court like a long tent of glass [111]. Paced in measures of eight feet, its sloped face assumes a slower rhythm than that of the colonnade opposite, where hollyhock columns almost eight feet tall are spaced only four feet apart [112]. The colonnade begins near a corridor that emerges from the servants' dining room to cross the court on square steps of cement tile [113]. The specifications for exterior walkways and steps at first called for flagstones, but were revised in favor of art-stone, a change that strengthened the character of the house and its consistency of expression. A small stream once curled be-

neath the steps to connect the circular pool with the luxuriant water garden. By forming a gallery, the colonnade redeems an otherwise mute north wall, affords a sheltered passage parallel to that of the pergola and shades the dining room from the glare of sunlight [114]. It also enhances the space and life of the court by generating an ornamental play of shadows. Finally, the colonnade creates a processional rhythm toward the stairs to the roof terraces [115].

The court stairs are a masterstroke, a great moment of the house [116]. They ascend toward the sky in playful grandeur, as if to lightly mimic the way to some remote and forgotten altar, and here Wright's command of scale becomes breathtaking. Six of the high-spirited finials can be seen at

112. Colonnade, looking northwest. Loggia shows changes made in 1947. (Ezra Stoller © Esto)

once. Invariably, they signal a flight of steps—just as the hollyhock patterns in the living-room rug in every instance climbed from one level to another.[11] The finials also rise as counterpoint to the predominantly horizontal character of the house. They sing to the sky, and populate the roof even when no one is there [117]. The roof terraces build their own sunny and buoyant world. Like the rooms below, they offer vistas inward to a self-sufficient place, but just as many outward to the city, the ocean and the hills [118].

[11] The two finials on the balcony of the owner's bedroom are not original; in a restoration priority list dated February 11, 1976, Lloyd Wright recommended they be removed. The small, masklike glyph on the face of each finial is the most overtly primitivist detail of the house (*see* fig. 25).

ABOVE: 113. Passage to servants' quarters, looking predominantly north. Water garden has been filled in. OPPOSITE, BOTTOM LEFT: 114. Colonnade, looking west. OPPOSITE, TOP: 115. Early view of garden court, looking predominantly west. OPPOSITE, BOTTOM RIGHT: 116. Stairs to roof terraces, looking northwest.

117. View from roof, looking southeast.

118. View from roof, looking north.

THE "PROUD AND BEAUTIFUL HOUSE"

ALINE BARNSDALL NEVER GAVE Hollyhock House a fair chance to become her home. She traveled more than ever. Disappointed by the cost of the house, she left for Europe even before work on it ceased in October 1921. Less than two years later, she asked Wright to design another house; and she thought about selling Olive Hill. Then she changed her mind. By the end of 1923, she was trying to give the highest part of the hill—along with Hollyhock House—to the City of Los Angeles.

Wright returned from Japan for the last time in 1922. Early the next year he established his studio in a rented house in west Hollywood. "The weather here is remarkably fine," he wrote Louis Sullivan on March 3, 1923. "Miss Barnsdall (of Olive Hill) has given me a new home to build for her at Beverly—on a beautiful twelve-acre mountain side—Mrs. Millard of Highland Park has given me another little studio house on a charming lot [in Pasadena]." In a note to Wright on June 8, Miss Barnsdall stated her terms for Olive Hill: $600,000 paid into escrow, $500,000 when escrow is completed, $700,000 within a year; the seller permitted the use of the house for 12 to 14 months. "Please don't argue it with me," she wrote. "I can take advice from nobody. I've been at it so long that I am temporarily tired & would prefer a few months in Europe." The next day, she turned to the project for her new house:

Enclosed you will find a check—the 5% payment on plans for my house which [is] to cost $125,000, this with the understanding that plans are to be made to fit a new site and certain changes made that I desire. I know that I shall want the house on a smaller scale with open loggias where now is solid concrete . . . You know what you call my weakness, which I call my strength, that I hate to part with money as long as it is not balanced by money coming in—that I will never borrow or jeopardize my father's fortune—and I know your weaknesses.

Let's be friends & get something done that can be a complete expression—even tho' it is smaller in scope than you dream & done a little at a time.

Soon she became preoccupied with other projects. One was finishing Hollyhock House; another, building a kindergarten she had asked Wright to design for a site on the west slope of Olive Hill. Sugartop was now six years old. In the fall of 1923, Miss Barnsdall grew concerned that Wright was ignoring the kindergarten project while he spent his time remodeling Residence "B," which he had rented from her as his new studio. In a letter of October 18 from Montreux, Switzerland, she wrote that her secretary reported nothing was happening with the schoolhouse:

Lang says that on Sept. 24th there were only a few stakes on the ground; but it is absolutely promised for December 10th . . . She says you're a genius and not to worry. I am inclined to be skeptical & suggest that you speed up your genius a bit—knowing how bad it is for the reputation of the school to have no permanent home . . . I would not have rented you the house but used it for the school, had you told me it would be so long building. I won't have the school go off from the hill, and as I start to finish the upper part of my own house as soon as I return it won't be possible to keep [the school] there—then Sugar needs her bedroom.

It has occurred to me lately that I am a slave to the idea of doing something beautiful—and not being really free. I am making *life* ugly by it—and life comes first. So I begin to practice the fine art of elimination and will do *nothing beautiful* or *otherwise* only as it enhances life for me. It doesn't enhance life for me to feel that you are putting the work on "B" before mine, knowing how it jeopardizes the beginning of the school . . . am willing to apologize if I find I am wrong. If I am not, God help the future of our work on the hill.

Wright spent much of that fall at Taliesin and in Chicago. Will Smith, his assistant, warned him from Los Angeles that the school would begin using his studio in Residence "B" by the middle of November. "A delightful prospect," Smith wired on November 9. "When do you return?" Miss Barnsdall sailed from Europe late that month. In December she was back in Los Angeles. So was Wright; but he soon took leave of Residence "B." Miss Barnsdall expressed surprise:

As usual there seems to have been a misunderstanding, as I had no idea you were to leave "B" until I received the note that you were going that day because you found it impossible to work there in the confusion . . . I sincerely hope you never rent a house from [me] again or any way do business outside of that as architect . . . I am so sure that you and I are only able to weave confusion just at present that I am eliminating [everything except] what must be done to pass this over to the city.

When she offered part of the hill to the city, Miss Barnsdall proposed that Hollyhock House become a branch library and its grounds a park. She would donate $5,000 toward buying new books, and would provide the house with an entrance for children and with more light and heat. There was some talk of using the house as a children's theater, a much better idea. Despite a great deal of publicity, the city council in March 1924 rejected the gift. Projected costs of maintaining the house and the park appear to have presented the major obstacle.[1]

Miss Barnsdall soon found that she and Wright worked

together no better when they were in Los Angeles than when they had been separated by oceans. She abandoned the kindergarten project after it had been started, and eventually gave up on her new house. As to Hollyhock House, she wanted to put bookcases in the music room and to remove the wall that separated the library from the living room; Wright did make drawings for a tall librarian's chair, a librarian's desk, four cane chairs, an overstuffed armchair like those in the living room and a stand for displaying her antique bas-relief from Tripoli. He also designed andirons and a fire-screen for the living room. Nothing was accomplished. Instead, Wright and Miss Barnsdall began another battle. Wright claimed architectural fees as well as compensation for what he spent in remodeling Residence "B" into his studio. Miss Barnsdall wrote him on January 21, 1924, that their working relationship was over. The "business outside of that as architect" in which Wright had been engaged for many years was selling art, particularly Japanese woodblock prints.[2] Miss Barnsdall contested the value of some prints he had conveyed to her:

I have called up your lawyer and he says he will send a representative . . . This settlement is made on the basis that there is no building to be done for or by us at any future time.

I can't return the screens until all adjustments are made. . . . One expert has told me the Japanese prints I took on the loan last spring were worth only $25 to $30 apiece . . . instead of the $120 you asked for them. That is the reason I want to make the exchange to the screen. I am afraid you were cheated on them.

By challenging Wright's eye for art, she merely reaped his fury. Within a few weeks, he began a legal maneuver: A sheriff's deputy awoke Miss Barnsdall to serve a summons, search the house and repossess the screens. She quickly posted a $10,000 bond and recovered them. A year later, Wright rekindled the dispute. She might be "meaner and trickier than anyone else," he wrote her from Taliesin on March 4, 1925, but he would retain Clarence Darrow to prosecute his case:

Both you and I, it seems, have had a dirty-linen washing in public coming to us for some time, and this will be it . . .

If I had not lost so much valuable time in crossing seas and continents on false alarms and had not had so much serious effort aborted by your interference and arbitrary

---

[1] Minutes of the Los Angeles Public Library Board for Dec. 8, 1923, Feb. 4, 1924 and Apr. 2, 1924; of the Board of Playground and Recreation Commissioners, Dec. 15, 1923; and of the Board of Park Commissioners, Dec. 18, 1923, Jan. 2, 1924, Feb. 27, 1924 and Apr. 15, 1924. *Also see* Norman M. Karasick, "Art, Politics, and Hollyhock House," M.A. thesis, California State University, Dominguez Hills, 1982.

[2] See Julia Meech-Pekarik, "Frank Lloyd Wright's Other Passion," in *The Nature of Frank Lloyd Wright*, ed. Carol R. Bolon, et al. (Chicago, 1988), pp. 125–153.

119. Early view from roof toward owner's bedroom, looking southeast; new window at right.

ignorance in depriving me of all responsibility for my own work, thereby aborting so much really great effort on my part in your behalf these past seven years, I wouldn't feel so bitter now. And if on top of that I hadn't been tricked out of six or seven thousand dollars in cash by my faith in your word I perhaps wouldn't start again even now—at that. Yet when I remember you have accused me of swindling you when I turned over to you rare things of rare value to any rare appreciation of beautiful works of Art, only to find your appreciation was only suspicious and common, and to find you in the "market" to "check up" on values that have none there nor ever could have had any—on things which that market cannot produce at any price unless by accident—then I would go on till I dropped or broke . . . So I am going on until it may be we'll both wish we had never been born.

Six weeks later, Wright telegraphed his attorney in Pasadena to suggest various lawsuits against his former client. "Barnsdall needs stick of dynamite," he wired on April 15. "Step on her." It was a bad time in Wright's life; litigation clouded both his professional career and his marital situation. The fight embittered Miss Barnsdall as well. In a letter of December 10, 1926, she looked back to her dream for Olive Hill:

I was fresh to a big enterprise and you did not protect me from my ignorance, rather you used it to project your own ideas . . .

It is I who has integrity toward the beautiful rather than you, who destroy your fine gifts with petty indirection. It went deeper than money, for it shocked me into fear of doing impulsive, generous things.

The dispute at last came to an end in January 1927 with a document that left undisclosed the terms of their settlement.

During this unhappy period, Miss Barnsdall turned to Schindler for help with Hollyhock House. In 1924 he designed some small brass shades for light fixtures. The next year he finished the upstairs bedrooms and the wardrobe. The cost of about $2,200 for the north chamber and $5,200 for the owner's suite reflected how little had been done with the second story in the summer of 1921. Schindler no longer served as an anonymous pencil in his master's hand; he no longer worked for Wright. He opened the west wall of the owner's room with a quirky, rhombus-shaped window embellished on the inside with a stationary wood grille [119].

He also designed a polygonal mural to ornament the austere fireplace, and some furniture that included another wood stand for the antique stone relief from Tripoli.

Schindler's changes encouraged Miss Barnsdall to think of even more radical alterations. In December 1925, she wrote him from Cortina d'Ampezzo, Italy:

> When I come home I want to turn the storage room into a semi-bedroom and sleeping porch for Sugartop in this way: opening it on the patio side above the stone work (Wright suggested doing this at one time himself, putting glass at each side so the pine woods could be seen thru—I don't want to do quite this) turning that long ugly passage into the room when the doors are open, covering the outside with a fine iron screen and the inside with glass folding doors, lifting the present floor of the room a step higher so it is like a platform to the hall, finishing the room in the form of a tent in white oak . . . In this way, Sugar will have a higher, dryer winter room . . . The floor raised a few inches and insulated will be warm, and with the entire west side opened and the small windows latticed and opened there will be light and air enough, don't you think? It will be much healthier to live upstairs in the winter, and I want Sugar safely screened in close to me so we won't need governesses and care takers. I have had strangers in my house for so many years that I long for the comfort of my own small family alone, as I am having it now. That arch way is an eyesore at present. I have other things in mind for later.

Schindler added light-boxes at the garden court and entrance loggia in the summer of 1926, but once again Miss Barnsdall was preparing to give Hollyhock House to the city. This time she succeeded; and she left the house before making such clumsy, incoherent changes as she had proposed in her letter from Italy. One of the great features—the bridge—seemed to her nothing but an "eyesore." She would have ruined it.

Barnsdall Park became a memorial to her father and a Christmas gift to the City of Los Angeles. In a deed of December 23, 1926, she donated Hollyhock House and about eight acres; the Board of Park Commissioners formally accepted the gift on January 3, 1927.[3] Miss Barnsdall intended the park for art and children, and the favorable influence of the one upon the other. The deed imposed several restrictions. To protect the view to the west, no structure was to be built more than 60 feet higher than Edgemont Street. The house was to be used by the California Art Club for at

least 15 years, and for art purposes forever after. Miss Barnsdall would provide a bronze relief sculpture to commemorate her father, but the park was to have no monuments or statues except those "in memory of artists, or in commemoration of art." As long as the house stood, its landscape scheme was to be maintained and renewed. (A survey dated May 10, 1927, identifies the olive trees, Monterey pines, eucalyptus trees, black acacias, oleanders, boxleaf asaras, mother ferns, fancy-leafed caladiums, sage rockroses, sky flowers, hybrid fuchsia, English ivy, Chinese hibiscus, Lombardy poplars, Australian ferns, California peppers, lilies, lilacs, periwinkles, sand verbenae and a few other plants.) Finally, the city was to keep the park in first-class condition.

Miss Barnsdall asked Ella Buchanan, a Los Angeles artist and member of the California Art Club, to create the memorial relief.[4] The plaque was mounted at the pool by the motor court, and it bore the inscription:

BARNSDALL PARK
in memory of
THEODORE N. BARNSDALL
1851–1917
Our fathers mined for the gold of this country
We should mine for its beauty.   ALINE BARNSDALL

In a second gift to the city, Miss Barnsdall on July 28, 1927, conveyed Residence "A" and several acres around it as additions to the park. The house was to be used chiefly for children's classes in the arts, she stipulated, and music was to be taught by the Dalcroze eurhythmic method for at least 12 years, or as long as she provided the teacher. (That fall, her daughter attended the Dalcroze School in Geneva, Switzerland.) Hollyhock House became the home of the California Art Club on August 31. Miss Barnsdall wrote to the membership:

> I would like this gift to grow like our own California oak—slowly, with its separate branches each reaching from the same trunk—the Art Club, the Recreation Center and finally my own theatre. In giving the park I have thought of my father, of the happiness of children and young people with Olive Hill as a place to work and play, a background for their dreams and memories, and my reluctance to see a building and landscaping of great beauty destroyed . . . No country can be great until the least of its citizens has been touched by beauty, truth

---

3 Deed No. 8658, recorded Jan. 7, 1927, in Book 4727, p. 60. It corrected an earlier deed of Oct. 30, 1926. Residence "A" and the land around it were added in Deed No. 9720, dated July 28, 1927.

4 Ella Buchanan (1869–1951) taught at the Art Institute of Chicago from 1911 to 1915, when she moved to Los Angeles. She also created a bas-relief portrait of Miss Barnsdall and, for the fountain pool by the exedra, a bronze dancing figure. See Sylvia Street, "Barnsdall Park, New Home of California Art Club," *California Graphic*, Apr. 2, 1927, p. 12.

and freedom; unless all three radiate from this little hill it is as nothing.[5]

Miss Barnsdall still talked about Wright's model for the theater, even though Norman Bel Geddes found the design unintelligent and unworkable, and the architect H. P. Berlage, as far away as Holland, described the project as one of "those designs which are pre-destined never to be executed."[6] If she held to a dream, her ambivalence was nonetheless apparent—as in an undated letter to Wright:

I have heard you criticize me—but that makes no difference—I also criticize you. I don't think you perfect as an architect any more than you have found perfection in me as a client—yet I would have no one else to build my theatre, and you will go a long way before you will find an *individual* more in sympathy with your work—it's easy to persuade sheep . . .

If you consider that you can work along *with me* in an orderly fashion, that will get us to [a] point that the world can see. Let's go ahead without comment—otherwise, I prefer giving up. My soul is worth more than a dozen damned theatres & this is doing terrible things to it.

Early in 1927, she wrote that she was prepared to put about $350,000 into the theater. Wright must not have been satisfied. Later that year, on October 3, he wrote her:

You have declared that money-considerations did not determine your motives, your affections nor your acts. But you should be measured and all your acts judged in connection with your money—because your money is a feature of your power and the character of any of your acts can only be seen in relation to that power you hold in your hands . . . I don't get you in regard to your money—at all.

Miss Barnsdall responded on November 16 from Valencia, Spain:

The great trouble has always been that your focus on me is distorted. I have always been a rich woman to you . . . Instead of facing the "power" of money, in the old sense, let us face the fact that the world must work toward a cleaner relation between money and art . . .

Life manages to gradually strip us of all we care about. I can never give very much to a world that puts my money before my energy & the original quality of my whole

being—but there are indications that these last are being glimpsed by some—& it is these few that will give me the impetus to get something beautiful done.

Wright had struck the nerve he no doubt aimed for. Miss Barnsdall could not easily reconcile her great wealth and style of living with her radical position in politics. In a second message to the Art Club, sent from a villa in Geneva, she virtually denied her most obvious claim to distinction:

My present feeling is opposed to the patronage of the arts by the rich. I was sorry to have to give in the way I did, though to me it was never so much giving as realizing an idea, and no theatre will be built until this same impersonal projection is assured. Patronage ruins artists as capitalism ruins living conditions for the many. Art can only be healthy when it is linked up in an impersonal way with the state, and independent of patrons.[7]

But she had other reasons for giving away Hollyhock House so soon after building it. The house was too large for her needs. She was spending more and more time in Europe, as she had before the war. Her pattern of living placed little value on a permanent home. Hollyhock House, moreover, was too quick to call for repairs. "You have forgotten a lot about that house in twenty years," she wrote Wright on August 9, 1943. "I spent almost $20,000 trying to make the roof stop leaking after your contractor gave up." An early aerial photograph records a pile of rubble—whether from work on the roofs, the loggia floor or both—and shows a higher coping and new roof on the breakfast room [*see* 50]. Rain also leaked into the living room from the leaded-glass skylight above the fireplace, poorly covered at the roof by the second skylight.

Wright did not easily accept blame. He mentioned the leaks in a letter he wrote Lloyd not long after Eric Lloyd Wright was born in November 1929:

Aline Barnsdall has never told anyone that she took the building of her house out of my hands and put it into the hands of her contractor, Robertson—in order to avoid what she finally got—a badly-built building. She has never applied to me to fix it for the same reason. I understand the place is going to hell now all around owing to the leaks. —She is declaring she can't live under an umbrella and so won't live in her houses and is going to buy one ready-made. I have to stand for her bullishness in trying to build her own place. Why not tell the truth herself.

But the ambiguous status of Robertson was an old issue.

5 "An Expression From Miss Barnsdall," *California Art Club Bulletin,* Aug. 1927.
6 H. P. Berlage, in *The Life-Work of the American Architect,* p. 84.

7 *California Art Club Bulletin,* May 1928.

120. Garden court about 1928, looking northwest.

Schindler soon became the new and mutually acceptable scapegoat. "Schindler and I are not speaking," Miss Barnsdall wrote Wright from London on November 5, 1930. "He can design but he can't build." Wright already suspected Schindler of trading on their association and exaggerating the work he had done as an assistant. When he answered Miss Barnsdall on November 18, Wright blamed the mishaps of Hollyhock House on Schindler *and* Robertson. "It was a transition building of great beauty and deserved a better fate," he wrote her. Later, in his autobiography, he asked: "I wonder if all buildings are not transition buildings in some sense if they are really great buildings? And always will be?"[8]

Why was the house so vulnerable to water? Wright gave one explanation in a letter he wrote Miss Barnsdall on May 28, 1943:

The worst feature of the house was always [the] lack of the intended roof. The roof was only temporary, waiting for the tile pavement that made the roof surfaces into terraces.

During all these years water has been sliding down the walls onto the sills . . . The roof has had only patchwork attention . . .

If you remember, the house had already cost so much you refused to go any further with it, declaring that you would leave it as it was. The main difficulties are due to that incomplete roof.

Miss Barnsdall told a different story. "I insisted upon starting the tiled roof," she wrote Wright on August 9, 1943, "but the side walls or something would not hold it, and I was told that the leakage was caused by the two materials, the side wall and concrete frieze, that would not fuse; they shrank in a different way . . . ."

Miss Barnsdall nonetheless had given the house to the city in good faith, and the California Art Club took pride in its new home [120]. Over the years, however, Hollyhock House suffered changes and faced threats beyond that of rain. Because of problems with the water course, particularly where it led under the loggia and living room, the water garden was forsaken and filled in with soil. The two guest rooms were obliterated to create an exhibition gallery. In the summer of 1929 a new gallery building was proposed for the south slope of the hill, and Miss Barnsdall even asked Wright if he would be interested in designing it; of course he was. Nothing came

of the proposal, but in 1932 a member of the Art Club advanced a more disturbing plan: to form a gallery by roofing the garden court and demolishing the pergola and colonnade. Lloyd Wright countered with plans of his own. He sent them to his father, who wrote Miss Barnsdall that an extension to the south would confuse the features of the house, but the garden court might well be closed with a hemicycle designed to preserve the vista of the pine trees above it. Nothing happened, but Miss Barnsdall kept in mind the notion of the hemicycle. During the later years of the Depression the house began to deteriorate; yet it stood intact [121].

After all their battles, Wright and Miss Barnsdall continued to correspond, and occasionally they met. Wright was usually at Taliesin. Miss Barnsdall wrote from New York, Paris, Athens, the Engadine in Switzerland or her home at Lake Arrowhead in California. Sometimes she stayed in Residence "B," which, after the fashion of Hollyhock House, she sometimes called Oleanders. In 1941 she wrote Wright to encourage his pacifism. In a letter of August 5, he responded, "I am glad we see together on this foolish push toward war." Then he turned to Hollyhock House:

Why can't we do something to complete and preserve the original Olive Hill Aline Barnsdall house? It was a true symphony and has already done a great work in the world in spite of its scandalous condition. It would be so easy to save it for a hundred years to come if you would cooperate. The house will always be associated with your name, world wide.

Miss Barnsdall, for the moment, was more interested in repairing Residence "B," where she meant to live again; the water had been shut off, and the walls were badly cracked. Wright visited the house in November 1941. He expressed surprise that the walls were built of hollow tile, not concrete, and he recommended that they be reinforced.

The city in March 1942 ordered the California Art Club to vacate Hollyhock House; the house was declared unsafe for public use and was closed. A city inspection had found damage to the foundations, mud sills, joists, girders, subfloors and studs from the action of termites, post beetles and dry rot.

"What has happened to *our* house?" Miss Barnsdall asked Wright in a letter of September 24, 1942. "You know that it has been condemned. Can nothing be done?" That fall she bought a house in Santa Fe, New Mexico, in a transaction that prompted the FBI to note that she paid $8,000 for it without bothering to look inside. Wright thought Hollyhock House was about to be demolished by the city, and he asked John Lautner, a former apprentice, to rescue the art-stone mural from the living room, some examples of the hollyhock

---

[8] Wright, *An Autobiography*, p. 225. Not many months later, Wright broke off all relations with Schindler; in a letter of June 19, 1931, he wrote Schindler: "You were, officially, superintendent for the Barnsdall houses, and a poor excuse for one, playing both ends against the middle all the time."

121. Garden court in 1939, looking east.

ornament and some panels of leaded glass. But the parks department was simply letting the house fall into ruin, with thoughts that after the war a new building could be constructed for no more than it would cost to repair the residence. Miss Barnsdall in 1943 grew increasingly suspicious of an intrigue to destroy the park and to prevent her from using Residence "B." She asked Wright how much it would cost to repair Hollyhock House. "I don't want the proud and beautiful house on the top of the hill to fall into miserable decay," she wrote on May 25, 1943. Wright answered three days later:

The Building Department has condemned the main residence on Olive Hill chiefly because the city wants to get rid of the house: termites and dry rot are the excuses. No doubt both are present but even so several thousand dollars would make the house better than it ever was . . .

Were the building made tight there would be no problem except to repair decay and use a proper insecticide against further damage by termites—all of which is not difficult.

Later that year, in November, he wrote her again to say that he would do anything he could "to save that fine work which you inspired and instigated." On December 2, she answered:

I don't think you quite understand what helping me means & it's not helping me to spend more money on the house—I was done with that long ago—but making it easier to have some group, preferably the government, know that there is a house being wasted and one particularly suited to teaching Arts & Crafts to discharged service men as they are doing in hospitals all over the country today: a ward of blocked glass built in a semicircle from kitchen unit to Betty's unit—in the circular garden—could take care of fifty injured service men, at least . . .

I consider that it was I & not the house that was sacrificed . . . I will explain when I see you.

So the hemicycle plan was revived, although never executed.9 The idea of making the residence into a center for war veterans, however, took life with Mrs. Dorothy Clune Murray of Los Angeles, whose son, Lt. James William Clune Jr., was killed in action in November 1944 in eastern France. She soon inspected Hollyhock House with Lloyd Wright, who wrote his father some months later:

A Mrs. Murray is attempting to interest the federal

government in taking over Olive Hill and having you put the house in the park in shape, all for use of soldier rehabilitation.

She's seen Aline, who wants two million dollars for the property [the remainder of the hill] and the right as Mrs. Murray says to sit in her wreck of a house on the side of the hill and raise hell generally. But Mrs. Murray thinks she can handle the matter—so am giving her what help I can.

Mrs. Murray hoped to lease the house from the city for ten years, Lloyd Wright wrote his father on June 5, 1945. "She expects to put some eight to ten thousand dollars into the rehabilitation of the building and an equal amount or more in furnishing the structure," he wrote. "What do you propose?" Lloyd Wright returned to the house at the end of September and found it a shambles. The parks department had stripped the trim and casework from the walls, scrambled the electrical system and removed much of the plumbing. Mrs. Murray nevertheless persisted with her plan to use the house as the Clune Memorial, dedicated to servicemen and the memory of those who gave their lives. During most of 1946, Lloyd Wright made drawings for what became in 1947 the first rebuilding of Hollyhock House. His work was subject to his father's suggestions and approval.

Many changes were made. By no means was the rebuilding conceived as a project in historic restoration. New stairs to new basement restrooms replaced the lavatory near the main entry. The simple wood grille at the entry was supplanted by a fussy screen of triangulated glass panes hung on metal struts. The kitchen was brought up to date. Cabinets were built into the west wall of the music room, which became the reception room. A desk was added to the breakfast room, now designated the office. A narrow opening was cut through the north wall of the living room for a fixed pane of glass, and a proper clerestory at last was constructed above the skylight to combat the leaks and glare of sunlight [122]. Trellis work was added to the east side of the loggia. Sash was removed from the pergola to make it an open gallery with trellises, and it was connected to the exhibition space through French doors. The transoms were removed from what had once been the north wall of the guest rooms, and the wall was filled in to the ceiling. Most of the playroom was turned into an open porch, with trellises again taking the place of glass.

As if in reprise of 1921, client and architect again clashed. Wright withdrew in May 1947; he told Mrs. Murray she had no idea of how to achieve a distinguished harmony, no feeling for the house as a work of art and no respect for an artist's integrity or devotion to an ideal. Lloyd Wright quit, too, as he wrote his father on June 4:

9 A plan-sketch catalogued as 1705.047 in the Frank Lloyd Wright Archives shows how easily the addition would fit the original pattern of semicircles at the east front of the house.

ABOVE: 122. Clerestory above living-room skylight, looking predominantly west.
RIGHT: 123. Catalogue to Lloyd Wright exhibition, 1966.

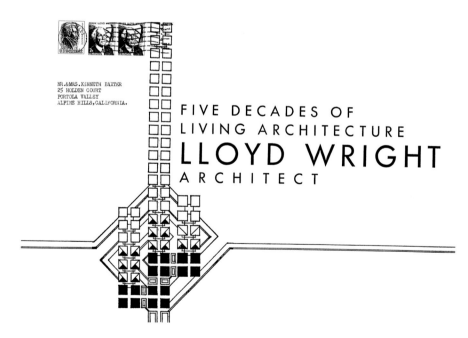

Checking on the work I had to complete, I found that while we were waiting for clarification of the situation, Dr. Chart had "decorated" one of the rooms—atrociously—painting walls in imitation of cold, cross-hatched cheap wallpaper—hideous color—and out of scale—Staining oak trim a greenish Grand Rapids finish as mean as Hades itself. It couldn't be worse.

Murray wants her pink exterior walls. The color we recommend she considers mud . . .

It is obvious why neither of us can, under the circumstances, do anything for that building.

Miss Barnsdall did not live to see the rebuilding of Hollyhock House. Had she ever understood the house? In a letter she wrote Wright from Santa Fe on June 4, 1946, she said she had just learned of his "especial interest in the Indian" by reading John Lloyd Wright's book *My Father Who Is on Earth*. "Living here," she wrote, "I am coming to feel that the Indian is our one classic tradition."

Alone with her pet dogs, Aline Barnsdall suffered a heart attack and was found dead in Residence "B" on December 18, 1946. In her will, she left $5,000 in trust for the care of her dogs, which were to be "maintained in comfort" until the last of them died. Although for years she had pretended to Wright that she had to count her pennies, her estate was appraised at more than $2 million. Her art collection, appraised at only about $100,000, numbered more than 160 works and included nine paintings by Monet, five by Renoir, three by Picasso, two by van Gogh and two by Gauguin.[10]

Residence "B" was demolished early in 1954. Wright returned to Hollyhock House that year and expanded the chain of animal pens into a temporary municipal art gallery for an exhibition of his work titled "Sixty Years of Living Architecture." It ran from June 2 through July 11. The catalogue included pictures of Hollyhock House, which Wright briefly described:

> . . . a characteristic California romanza, embodying the characteristic features of the region for a client who loved them and the theater. She named the house Hollyhock House and asked that the flower be used as a motive in the decoration of the place. The wooden structure of the period and place plastered with concrete and trimmed with cast stone.

In 1957, two years before his death, Wright prepared a master plan for Barnsdall Park that envisioned a large municipal art gallery east of Hollyhock House.[11]

Elsewhere in Los Angeles, in the summer of 1966, Lloyd Wright exhibited his own work under the title of "Five Decades of Living Architecture." So attached was he to his father, he showed the wash drawings he had made for Miss Barnsdall some 45 years earlier, and for the cover of the catalogue used a graphic motif much like an ornament from Hollyhock House; he mailed a copy to his sister Catherine with the Frank Lloyd Wright postage stamps first issued on June 8 of that year in Spring Green, Wisconsin [123].

A substructure investigation of Hollyhock House in May 1967 found substantial termite and dry-rot damage at the entry hall, music room, west part of the living room, gallery, child's room, nursemaid's room and servants' rooms. In 1967–70 the parks department carried out a second rebuilding. Much of the floor system was replaced. So was the lintel over the south living-room door. The trellis along the east side of the entrance loggia was reconstructed, as was the roof of the colonnade. The facing of the porte-cochere canopy was replaced. Exterior walls and many of the hollyhock ornaments were repaired.

Lloyd Wright returned to the house once again in 1974–75, now with his son Eric Lloyd Wright, to direct a restoration for which the city spent more than $500,000. He modestly reversed many of the changes he and his father had made in 1947, in order to take the house nearer to its original design. In a memorandum of September 1975—by now, he was 85 years old—he lamented the loss of the original landscaping:

> Decade after decade, due to neglect or butchery, the beautiful vines and hedges were allowed to die or were removed with their lovely South Sea Island blooms that the Polynesians of the Islands wore in their hair. Miss Barnsdall loved the color and romance of it and saw to it that similar color and flowering plants were used in the planting of the park, and so it was planted luxuriantly.[12]

The fragrance of Hollyhock House in its prime was caught with sympathetic grace in a suite of dreamy, soft-focus images by the Los Angeles photographer Viroque Baker [124, 125].

---

[10] Much of her art collection was on loan to the Los Angeles County Museum from 1940 to 1948. It was appraised in May 1947. The will and associated documents are filed as probate case No. 264062, the Superior Court of Los Angeles County.

[11] For the master plan and a perspective drawing, see Bruce Brooks Pfeiffer, *Frank Lloyd Wright Drawings* (New York, 1990), pp. 156–157. The present Municipal Art Gallery, not designed by Wright, was opened in 1971. It also houses the Gallery Theater. Residence "A," remodeled, serves as the Arts and Crafts Center, and the Junior Arts Center occupies a separate building.

[12] Lloyd Wright died in May 1978 at the age of 88. His father had died at 91 in April 1959. The landscape survey of May 1927 could guide a restoration of the grounds to their original luxuriance.

Norman Bel Geddes said that in 1916, the year Miss Barnsdall opened her Los Angeles Little Theatre, the mere mention of California stirred visions of sunshine and paradise. Frank Lloyd Wright arrived in Los Angeles to face great challenges. What could be a valid architecture for this romantic place? How could it be indigenous, non-European? Could this house for a woman who loved the theater somehow surpass stagecraft in overcoming the distinction between makebelieve and reality? If romance in architecture meant the freedom to create significant form governed only by a sense of proportion, could the house achieve the abstract pattern and rhythm of music? Could it be an invention, a work of high spirit and principle?[13]

Hollyhock House survives as the most significant residence from his middle years. It stands as his noble response to all those questions [126].

[13] The aura of stagecraft, especially in the garden court, has been emphasized by Elpidio Rocha in several conversations. Wright's longings for the freedom of music may have been encouraged by the celebrated remark of Walter Pater ("All art constantly aspires towards the condition of music") in *The Renaissance* (London and New York, 1890), p. 144, as well as the fact that Goethe called architecture "petrified music" (music in stone, not "frozen" music); see J. P. Eckermann, *Conversations of Goethe* (London, 1883), p. 378. The critic Clive Bell, in *Art* (London, 1913), *passim*, used the phrase "significant form" to describe what he considered the one quality common to all works of art.

124. Early view of west front, looking northeast.

125. Early view of living room, library and south terraces, looking east.

126. Hollyhock House, looking southeast. (Ezra Stoller © Esto)

INDEX

Page numbers in *italics* refer to illustrations only.